D1402611

Through God's Eyes

A Bible Study of God's Motivations for Missions

Through God's Eyes

A Bible Study of God's Motivations for Missions

William Carey Library
Pasadena, CA

Patrick O. Cate

© Copyright 2004 by Patrick O. Cate

All Rights Reserved

No part of this publication may be reproduced, stored in a retrieval system, or transmitted in any form or by any means—electronic, mechanical, photocopy, recording, or any other—without written permission of the publisher.

Scripture quotations marked (NIV®) are taken from the HOLY BIBLE, NEW INTERNATIONAL VERSION®. NIV®. Copyright © 1973, 1978, 1984 by International Bible Society. Used by permission. All rights reserved worldwide.

Cover design by Byron Barnshaw, layout by Karen Brightbill, editing by Nancy Maurer

Published by   **William Carey Library**
P.O. Box 40129
Pasadena, California 91114
(626) 720-8210
inquiries@wclbooks.com
www.wclbooks.com

ISBN 0878083596

Printed in the United States of America.

Table of Contents

What Many are Saying About
Through God's Eyes
A Bible Study of God's Motivations for Missions

Ted Barnett, U.S. Director—Africa Inland Mission

> "I would highly recommend the study, *Through God's Eyes* to every Christian who wants to understand God's passion for the world and how a believer can join God in responding to God's passion and man's needs."

Robert A. Blincoe, U.S. Director—Frontiers

> "You knew someone would put into your hands a dazzling, interactive study of the whole Bible in a way that reveals God's will for you. This book is it. Pat Cate is your mentor in this fact-filled, highly readable missions manual."

Jonathan Bonk, Executive Director—Overseas Ministry Study Center

> As a uniquely clear, concise, inductive overview of the Christian mission that is both current and biblically rooted, the book will at once inform and engage undergraduate and adult Sunday School students, familiarizing them with both theoretical and practical dimensions of the Church's missionary task."

Robert C. Booker, Vice President—New Brunswick Bible Institute

> "*Through God's Eyes* is a refreshing workbook on what missions is all about. I was pleased and impressed with the clarity, straightforwardness, and scriptural accuracy with which it was written. This could very well be the textbook/workbook I've been looking for in my introduction to missions classes."

Evvy Hay Campbell, Missions Professor—Wheaton Graduate School

> "With sterling quotes, graceful photographs and meaty resource materials, Pat Cate has given us an attractive tool for exploring missions in a fresh way. I warmly recommend this thoughtful, substantive guide."

David Chow, Executive Director—Ambassadors for Christ

> "I appreciate your work *Through God's Eyes*. It is interesting, informative and inspirational. I highly recommend this exciting in-depth study of foundational truth on missions."

Lyle W. Dorsett, Professor of Evangelism, Wheaton Graduate School

> "Pastors should read this refreshing book on the biblical bases of missions. Once pastors go through Cate's book they will want their parishioners to work through it. If this happens, we will see a revival in fervor for missions."

Hans Finzel, President—CBInternational

> "*Through God's Eyes* is designed to help believers discover God's passion for the world and what part He may want them to serve in it. I recommend it to seminaries and colleges who may want to use it as a basis for their Introduction to Missions or Biblical Theology of Missions course; mission boards who may want to ask their candidates or appointees to work through it as well as churches who may find it foundational for their short-term or long-term missionaries."

David P. Harvey, Associate Professor of Missiology—Toccoa Falls College

> "Dr. Cate has provided teachers of missions theology a plethora of penetrating questions which go to the core of theological issues needing answers today. Any serious student desiring to understand God's motivations for missions needs to delve deeply into this well-planned and challenging book. One of the more

difficult tasks of a professor of missions is the formulation of pertinent questions which are able to stir serious minds in terms of relevant questions of today. Patrick Cate has provided a wealth of material to help any missions professor in this endeavor.

Throughout this text of penetrating questions concerning God's motivations for missions, Dr. Cate has interwoven quotes from past and present mission leaders. These quotable quotes alone are worth the price of the book! This text of questions, quotes and up-to-date missions statistics is a welcome addition to any serious student's library. The "Suggestions for Further Reading" section provides an invaluable guide to a greater understanding of most missions topics from anthropology to missions theology, from missions web-sites to world religions. An excellent contribution to a serious study of God's plan for the nations."

Howard Hendricks, Distinguished Professor, Chairman, Center for Christian Leadership—Dallas Theological Seminary

"Two kinds of people live in our world- ones who say, "Here I am," and those who say, "There you are." Pat Cate is definitely a there-you-are person whose driving ambition is to dispatch good news about God's love to those who have no hope. Many believers agree that linking biblical truth with listening ears is the basic mandate of the Christian faith, but few understand its critical significance. *Through God's Eyes* is a front seat on a spectacular literary safari hosted by a missionary statesman who will change forever how you see our world.

John A. Huffman, Jr.—Senior Pastor, St. Andrews Presbyterian Church, Newport Beach, CA

"I have known Patrick Cate since our college years and have always been impressed with his passion for world missions. *Through God's Eyes* is a superb book/workbook/bibliography enabling the sincere Christ follower to understand more clearly God's biblical mandate for global evangelization. It is solid teaching combined with thought-stimulating, creative questions with helpful pictures, charts, statistics, quotes and even a touch of humor. This is a must resource for all of us to take seriously Christ's Great Commission."

Oli G. Jacobson, Chairman/CEO—New Tribes Mission

"*Through God's Eyes* gives Christians the opportunity to discover God's answers to their mission questions for themselves. Patrick Cate has given the Church an excellent tool for both personal and small group Bible studies that will yield eternal fruit in terms of personal growth, mission effort and souls saved."

Joe Jordan, Executive Director—Word of Life Fellowship

"Pat Cate has provided a challenging study guide for the biblical mandate to 'go ye into all the world.' Combining motivational quotes, historic illustrations and current statistics, he guides the reader through an inductive study of biblical passages calling us to be ambassadors for Christ, especially in the regions beyond our comfort zone."

Bob Kennedy, Academic Dean—Michigan Theological Seminary

"Pat Cate's Bible study, *Through God's Eyes*, is an excellent tool for motivating individuals, small groups and churches for missions. Step-by-step it lays the foundations for missions in the Scriptures and then moves our eyes to what God is doing around the world. It is an indispensable tool in mobilizing the Body of Christ for missions and the result of numerous years of actual ministry experience."

D. James Kennedy, Senior Minister—Coral Ridge Presbyterian Church, Ft. Lauderdale, FL, Founder of Evangelism Explosion International

"*Through God's Eyes* is a fine inductive study for individuals or groups on the biblical meaning, motives and message of the Church for World missions. Rediscover through this study of God's word and World Missions statistics what made the early church tick and become animated like them to turn the world upside down."

Woodrow Kroll, President—Back to the Bible

> "What a breath of fresh air for missions. In *Through God's Eyes*, Dr. Pat Cate uses an interactive method of getting us into God's Word for the answers that everybody is asking about missions. Pat doesn't need to give us the answers; he directs us to God's answers. *Through God's Eyes* is an easy-to-use guide to the heart of what missions is all about. Every Christian needs to see the world through God's eyes."

John Kyle, Sr. Senior Vice President—Evangelical Fellowship of Mission Agencies (EFMA), formerly Director of Urbana conventions.

> "*Through God's Eyes* is a comprehensive Bible study on world missions which is based on the Scriptures. Each part of the study is enhanced by appropriate quotations of Christian leaders as well as excellent cartoons. The one pursuing this study will be challenged to consider what their personal response will be to Jesus Christ's Great Commission."

Warren Larson, Director of the Zwemer Center for Muslim Studies—Columbia International University

> "The greatest feature of this study is that it gets people into the Bible and demonstrates that missions is God's idea—not our's. Other attractive qualities include the emphasis on church planting, and it presents facts, figures and numerous charts on how Muslims, for example, have been neglected in Christian missions. I highly recommend it."

Elizabeth Lightbody, EdD—Moody Bible Institute

> "Each lesson allows the learner to investigate the scriptural bases of God's heart for His world. The format of the book moves the reader from the Biblical mandate of mission into asking themselves key questions of application. I believe this material will serve as an effective tool in Biblical studies from teens through adults."

Michael G. Loftis, President—Association of Baptists for World Evangelism

> "I agree strongly with your premise—the Word of God is the key to the call of God into the world. Thanks for taking the time to put this Bible study on paper as a tool for the Holy Spirit's work in human hearts."

David Lundy, International Director—Arab World Ministries

> "In the Perspectives tradition, *Through God's Eyes* covers the broad sweep of missions in a hands-on way that will attract a wider range of people exploring the world of missions."

Don McCurry, President—Ministries to Muslims, Director of Ibero-American Institute of Transcultural Studies

> "Patrick Cate has come out with a workbook on missions that many of us wish we had written. The steady stream of study questions on the Word of God, the great quotes and illustrations and the exceptional segmented and extensive bibliography makes this an outstanding study for all interested in missions."

Paul McKaughan, President—Evangelical Fellowship of Mission Agencies (EFMA)

> "I found *Through God's Eyes* a wonderfully interactive guided tour of key foundational issues in missions today. Too often we look only at the pragmatics of mission and do not go back to the basic truths about God and His plan that form our motivations and mandate for mission. Just as the Lord has blessed the material in your training courses, I know that He will bless this material in it's broader circulation."

A. Scott Moreau, Chair and Professor of Missions and Intercultural Studies—Wheaton College, Editor, Evangelical Missions Quarterly

> "I could use many adjectives to describe *Through God's Eyes*: rich, rewarding, challenging, fresh, funny, personal, uncompromising, and—perhaps most important—thoroughly biblical. In it Pat Cate offers material that is accessible to the beginner and still challenging to those who are farther along the road in missions. My own missionary zeal was renewed, and I trust that you will be stimulated to be involved in God's work

among the unreached as a result of working your way through the scriptural foundations made available through this valuable resource."

Harold Netland, Professor of Philosophy of Religion and Intercultural Studies—Trinity Evangelical Divinity School

"In *Through God's Eyes* Dr. Patrick Cate combines a solid understanding of God's Word with many years of experience in intercultural missions to provide a very helpful and readable introduction to God's global purposes for humankind and our place in God's program. One's understanding of God's Word and the world will be challenged and enriched through this study."

Mikel Neumann, Associate Professor of Missiology—Western Seminary

"I would use this book in the small groups of any church as well as in the thriving house church movements. It would be the ideal place to take the time and effort to help the many people coming into the church, as well as those long time Christians, to understand the foundational biblical basis for Global Mission."

Marvin J. Newell, Professor of Intercultural Studies—Moody Graduate School

"This insightful and methodical study into the major foundational issues facing missions today is written in an easy to understand format that can be used in a variety of teaching settings. Full of up-dated statistics and appealing graphics, Dr. Cate presents missions in a manner that is relevant and appealing. This is an excellent study for those who are just beginning to investigate missions, or for those who find the need for an up-dated review."

D. Jim O'Neill, President—UFM International

"Christians don't always 'get it.' What is it they don't get? Somehow Christians miss the great missional intent of the Scriptures. The danger is that we conclude the Bible is all about 'me.' Pat Cate's study, *Through God's Eyes*, will not allow you to draw such conclusions. For the serious student who works through the text your efforts will be richly rewarded with an understanding of God's heart for all peoples, a theology to undergird it and practical action steps to help you implement. I highly recommend this resource. May your heart be aflame for God and His world as a result of reading this book."

John H. Orme, Executive Director—Interdenominational Foreign Mission Association (IFMA)

"Instead of just talking about mission, this workbook gets you involved in the Scriptures. The studies lead to a personal response to the issues of lostness, the gospel, prayer, Christ's return, unreached people and the establishing of a church. This excellent study does not allow mere "commenting and counting," but leads to "doing and going.""

Greg H. Parsons, General Director—U.S. Center for World Mission

"*Through God's Eyes* captures the essence of both the key Biblical passages as well as core global issues in a unique way. The study walks you through dozens of issues in the scriptures and in your own life. Do this study with others, but be careful, it will change your life."

F. Douglas Pennoyer, Dean of Intercultural Studies—Biola University

"Thank you for your booklet. I enjoyed your adaptation of scriptural principles and diagrams, and even the comical illustrations."

Carol Potratz, Associate Director- NAB International Missions

"Pat Cate helps us seriously consider missions from God's perspective. The easy part of missions is packing your bag …the challenge is to prepare your heart. *Through God's Eyes* helps us to do just that …to open our heart and ponder God's call to us—then, pursue our place in His larger picture."

Richard Ramesh, Professor—Dallas Theological Seminary, President RREACH International

> "A self-guided tour to lay an epistemological foundation for global missions! How we know what we know concerning the realities of the unreached must be viewed through God's eyes—as found in the Bible. You will be increasingly convinced of oughtness.—in personal responsibility as you work through this manual."

James Raymo, USA Director—WEC International

> "I appreciated the sweep and breadth of *Through God's Eyes*. I felt something of the breadth of the Perspectives course interjected with creative humor and biblical insight. The interactive Q and A format would be very suitable for missions committees, study groups and anyone open to enlarging their vision of God's heart for the world."

Stephen L. Richardson, U.S. Director—Pioneers

> "Pat Cate's panoramic investigation of God's redemptive agenda has the potential to revolutionize your understanding of the scriptures and of your own life mission. This book is an important starting point for any world Christian or Christian worker."

Bong Rin Ro, President—International College and Graduate School, HI

> "This workbook has excellent graphs, pictures and statistics of missions which I wholeheartedly recommend to pastors and seminaries. I am planning to use this book as a textbook the next time I teach Introduction to Missions. For understanding the biblical principles for missions and present issues in missions, this book is on top!"

Ben Sells, Director—International Center for Excellence in Leadership, Coordinator, Missionary Learning Center International Mission Board, SBC

> "It's been said that 'God can't lead you based on what you don't know.' Studying *Through God's Eyes* helps the reader know a great deal more about God, his Word and his world. As a result, expect God to lead you in further discovering your strategic role of Kingdom advancement."

Jeff Seume—President, Tyndale Theological Seminary, The Netherlands

> "Dr. Pat Cate has produced an excellent work, *Through God's Eyes*, which will be used by the Lord to challenge His people to deepen their commitment to missions. Individuals and churches will grow in their understanding of the biblical basis for missions and the key issues facing the missionary enterprise today as they work through this study. I heartily recommend Dr. Cate's study to you as one which will enable all to catch God's and the author's, passion for missions."

Frank Severn, Director Emeritus—SEND International

> "Here is the 'tool' I have been looking for! *Through God's Eyes* is thoroughly biblical and intensely practical. It is a missions curriculum in one book! Thank you, Dr. Cate, for providing this for all of us who are seeking to 'declare God's glory to the nations.'"

Samuel Shahid, Professor of Islamic Studies—Southwestern Baptist Theological Seminary

> "I read your manuscript and I found it very practical and well organized. I was impressed with its methodology and the charts you included. The questions you designed are very helpful in guiding the students to find the facts by themselves. Also it encourages the students to diligently memorize the biblical verses. I really do encourage those who are interested in reaching out to the unreached or in discipling others to use it as an important source of study."

Alex G. Smith, Minister-at-Large (Buddhist World Focus)—OMF International

> "Pat Cate's workbook, *Through God's Eyes*, is a valuable, practical tool for discussing motivation and mobilization in mission. Being filled with inductive questions makes it an excellent aid for discerning God's heartbeat in the post-modern context today. All serious students, Sunday school teachers, pastors and potential cross cultural workers should study it carefully."

Tom Stallter, Chair, Department of Intercultural Studies and World Missions—Grace Theological Seminary

> "I find this workbook an excellent approach to the introduction to mission combined with a passion for the world. This workbook leads the student to discover answers to the most foundational, as well as the most burning issues in mission, and what a student discovers on his own he will never forget. The use of discovery will give the student ownership of the concepts and passion for the task God has given us. The topics covered are, without question, the central issues we must face, and in facing them as Pat has done here, we cannot come away without a greater commitment and a deeper passion."

James J. Stamoolis, Consultant to Educational and Missionary Organizations

> "Marvelous study guide that leads the reader into an understanding of God's plan for the nations to hear the message of redemption in Christ. Should be required reading in every Christian college and seminary."

Tom A. Steffen, Professor, School of Intercultural Studies—Biola University

> "A penetrating, provocative primer that will effectively help persuade potential candidates to participate in short- and long-term global missions."

Steve Strauss—SIM USA

> "In *Through God's Eyes* Pat Cate turns his readers to the Bible to dig out a biblical theology of missions for themselves. Any book that stimulates personal Bible study and awakens believers to God's heart for the world throughout Scripture is a good book. *Through God's Eyes* does both."

George Verwer—Founder of Operation Mobilization

> "What a great study. How can we get people into it? My prayer is that many will go the extra mile to get people into this important Bible study."

Timothy M. Warner, Ambassador-at-Large for Freedom in Christ Ministries

> "Based on years of scholarly study and of practical experience, Pat Cate has given us a guide to lead the earnest seeker to the biblical approach to missionary motivation. In a culture that tends to see things primarily from a cognitive or psychological perspective, he leads us to the intimate relationship with the Father Himself that leads us to see the world as He sees it."

John Watters, Executive Director—Wycliff Bible Translators International

> "May God use this Bible study to challenge many to engage in missions! Pat Cate starts us where all missions must begin—God, His love for humanity and the preservation of His glory. The study rightfully keeps Jesus Christ at the center of mission, and reminds us of those whom God called into mission in the past—our spiritual forebears. He then brings the study home to our own lives that we might consider what God is calling each of us to do. May we listen well to God's voice as we learn of His heart for the peoples of the earth!"

Daniel Wicher, President—CAM International

> "The multifaceted challenge of Christ's Great Commission includes the evangelism of the unreached, the training of believers to obediently follow Christ and the establishment of local churches among all ethnic peoples of the earth. Dr. Cate has provided a helpful study that focuses upon the urgent task of reaching the lost through the purposeful spreading of the gospel among all ethnic peoples today."

Ralph D. Winter, President, Professor of History—William Carey International University, Founder of the US Center for World Mission and the Perspectives on the World Christian Movement course

> "Surprising: A busy, veteran mission executive, both an advanced scholar and an activist, has taken the time to produce a first rate workbook/introduction to the cause of missions. Its keen content is beautifully and graphically laid out. There is nothing else like it."

J. Dudley Woodberry, Dean Emeritus and Professor of Islamic Studies—Fuller Theological Seminary

> "At a time when the vision for missions of many Christians has been clouded by contemporary pluralist ideas, Pat Cate helps us see the relevant scripture *Through God's Eyes* so that our hearts may beat with His and our feet may follow the path He shows us."

Through God's Eyes

A Bible Study of God's Motivations for Missions

We are glad you are open to investigating God's passion for this world. We will be observing a variety of motivations for missions given by our Lord in His Word. Clarity of motivation is essential for accomplishing any worthwhile challenge. Understanding the answer to the "why" question helps us get on the right track and keeps us there until we arrive where God wants us. This study also touches on several questions many of us have when we consider missions. We invite you to invest prayerful effort looking up each Scripture passage and thinking through your answers and applications.

There is a pure joy in discovering God's Word yourself and not letting a commentary or another person predigest it first. So this study is designed to bring you into the Word personally, to discover inductively what God is saying in Scripture and hopefully to help you gain a better sense of His direction for your own life. If you are a serious seeker, who wants to "love the LORD your God with all your heart, soul, mind and strength," you can find fuel for your love of God. Take whatever time is needed for each passage. Pray and meditate on each answer. You may want to mark or underline portions of Scripture where God is speaking to you.

You will find two kinds of questions, those whose answers are fairly clear in the text and questions which will require more meditation and prayer to understand what response God may want for you to take.

Like other worthwhile ventures, this study will take time, effort and persistence. This is a major in-depth study for the serious inquirer about missions. It will not be easy or quick, just as learning another language on the mission field will not be easy or quick. But God is quite able to help us do both. Many have found this study challenging but well worth the effort. Your work may yield significant profit as you study to better know the heart of God for this world and His guidance for your life. Be in prayer as you seek God's will through this study of the Bible. A wide variety of God's servants who have preceded us in His service share some of what they have learned throughout these pages. A wise step in missions is to learn from those who have gone before us, building on their shoulders.

> Nothing is particularly hard if you divide it into small jobs.
>
> —Henry Ford[1]

You may like to do one question, one page or one section per day until you have finished it. You may find it profitable to work through this study in your devotions, listening to God at the beginning or end of each day. Many groups spread the work of each chapter over several weeks. Link sausage can be cut at the links or any place in between. You still get sausage. This study also may be divided to fit your needs.

We trust this study will help you seek God's will for your own life, as well as help you to help others who are seeking God's will for their future. Feel free to use this study with a small group, Sunday school, college or seminary class. Discussion of your answers and observations with others who are also working their way through Through God's Eyes can increase the value of the study. *Through God's Eyes* can function as part of a course covering an introduction to missions or a biblical theology of missions. Some churches and missions require this study before they send their missionaries to the field, even for short-term mission trips. It is part of their required curriculum.

Each chapter includes reflection questions in the conclusion plus a relevant verse or verses for memorization. Take some time to meditate on both. Memorization, though difficult, can help us to value what God values. When Christ was tempted, He immediately gave Satan four passages which He had previously memorized and Satan left Him.

The primary sources of most statistics are:

Barrett, David B. and Johnson, Todd M. "Annual Statistical Table on Global Mission: 2004." International Bulletin of Missionary Research 28 (January 2004): 24-25.

Barrett, David B. and Johnson, Todd M. World Christian Trends AD30-AD2200: Interpreting the Annual Christian Megacensus Pasadena, CA: William Carey Library, 2001.

Guthrie, Stan. Missions in the Third Millennium: 21 Key Trends for the 21st Century. Waynesboro, GA: Paternoster Press, 2000.

Johnstone, Patrick and Mandryk, Jason. Operation World, 21st Century Edition Waynesboro, GA: Paternoster USA, 2001.

Welliver, Dotsey and Northcutt, Minnette, eds. Mission Handbook: U.S. and Canadian Protestant Ministries Overseas 2004-2006, 19th ed. Wheaton: Evangelism and Missions Information Service, Billy Graham Center, 2004.

Winter, Ralph D. and Hawthorne, Steven C. Perspectives on the World Christian Movement: A Reader, 3rd ed. Pasadena, CA: William Carey Library, 1999.

Quotations by some of God's wonderful servants relevant to God's motivations for missions, are spread throughout the study. A brief biographical sketch of each is included in the appendix. The biblical study of missions faces very serious issues. Yet God is also the author of laughter. A number of cartoons are enclosed to encourage a merry heart.

I am happy to hear your response to this study, what God has taught you through it and/or any suggestions for improvements in the next edition at <Pat@Christar.org>.

Roots

Few enterprises are the sole work of one person. This study is no exception. For over a decade hundreds of students of missions have worked through earlier renditions of Through God's Eyes and sent their valuable suggestions for improvement. Many of those suggestions have been incorporated.

Dr. Howard Hendricks, my first teacher of inductive Bible study, instilled a love for digging out what God is saying from the Word. Dr. and Mrs. Earle Cairns encouraged the writing process. Mrs. Jerrie Eshbaugh and Mrs. Barbara Cunnius, my administrative assistants, have kindly typed and retyped numerous revisions. Mary Ann Seume Cate, my ministry partner and sweetheart, has patiently endured many hours of study and revision.

My prayer is that God will use this process of exploring, digging, praying and thinking about the Word and the world so the next generation of world Christians will more clearly understand and fervently serve God's global purposes. We serve a wonderful LORD on behalf of very needy people.

Pat Cate

Patrick Cate

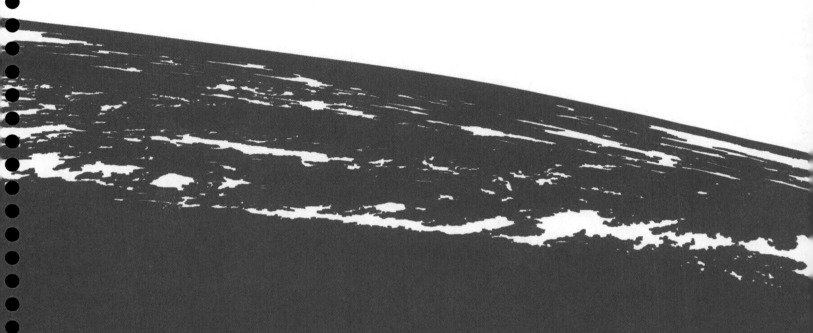

Chapter 1

To God Be the Glory

1. To God Be the Glory

The glory of God and Missions

Missions begins with God Himself. God has a passion that He be glorified and honored by all people groups on earth. But Satan and his forces have stolen some of the glory which belongs to God alone. God wants to restore His creation to His original purposes.

Is there any thing in your relationship with God that you wish you could tell the whole world? If so, what?

A. What is God's purpose for all the nations of the earth in Psalm 86:9?

B. What does the Psalmist exhort us to do with His glory in Psalm 96:3?

C. Meditate on Isaiah 40:3-15. Why is God able to reach His ultimate mission purposes without us humans?

D. Why do you think God has chosen to use humans (II Corinthians 4:7-12; 5:14-21)?

E.   Why has God created us according to II Corinthians 3:18 and Ephesians 1:4-6, 11-14? (See also Isaiah 43:7.)

F.   What does "glory" mean to you?

A dictionary may use "radiant splendor" as a definition of glory. The root meaning comes from "weight" or the weight of importance. It clearly includes "reputation." Part of glorifying God is to lift up His reputation.

What does "the glory of God" mean to you?

Based on Psalm 96, what does God want you to do about His glory and reputation in all the earth? (Gentiles, nations and people groups can have the same meaning in the original Hebrew.)

Understanding and valuing the glory of God can bring us to worship the Lord and to spread the worship of Him among all peoples.

"I trust your hearts are keenly focused on what the Lord has to say to us this evening, and not on the Lions' stinking loss to the Bears this afternoon on that lousy holding penalty call by the refs with 1:15 to go in the game!"

© 1997 Jonny Hawkins. Used by Permission.

> Missions is not the ultimate goal of the church. Worship is. Missions exists because worship doesn't. Worship is ultimate, not missions, because God is ultimate, not man. When this age is over, and the countless millions of the redeemed fall on their faces before the throne of God, missions will be no more. It is a temporary necessity. But worship abides forever.
>
> Worship, therefore, is the fuel and goal in missions. It's the goal of missions because in missions we simply aim to bring the nations into the white-hot enjoyment of God's glory. The goal of missions is the gladness of the peoples in the greatness of God ...
>
> But worship is also the fuel of missions. Passion for God in worship precedes the offer of God in preaching. You can't commend what you don't cherish.
>
> —John Piper[2]

> Carey and thousands like him have been moved by the vision of a great and triumphant God. That vision must come first. Savoring it in worship precedes spreading it in missions. All of history is moving toward one great goal, the white-hot worship of God and His Son among all the peoples of the earth. Missions is not that goal. It is the means. And for that reason it is the second greatest human activity in the world.
>
> —John Piper[3]

G. What is God's response to idolatry (Isaiah 42:8; 44:6-23)?

What does idolatry do to God's reputation?

We may think that we are not tempted to worship idols, but according to Colossians 3:5, what is greed or covetousness?

H. What place does the cross of the Lord Jesus Christ have in your glory or boasting? (Feel free to see how it affected Paul in Galatians 6:14.)

I. What is the relationship you observe between zeal for the glory of God and missions to the nations in Romans 15:4-21? (Gentiles, nations and people groups can also have the same meaning in the original Greek.)

J. Humanism exalts or worships man. Materialism makes the ultimate passion of life the acquisition or possession of material, temporal things. Buddhism calls for the worship of the man, Buddha, and ancestors, yet many Buddhists say there is no God. Hindus worship many idols including the peacock, cow, monkey, cobra and elephant. Many professing Christians also worship the wrong things such as freedom, democracy, things, power, sex, pride or family.

    Many Muslims worship at the graves of their saints, believing special power, answers to prayer and blessings come through the graves. Most Muslims believe in salvation by works, not grace and they reject the deity of Christ, the sonship of Christ, the crucifixion, resurrection, Trinity and the reliability of the Bible today.

    What glory is given to God through humanism, materialism, Buddhism, Hinduism and Islam based on Romans 1:21-25?

    What do religious substitutes do to the glory of God?

K. How would it glorify God for the gospel to be preached and lived out among these types of people, for the Holy Spirit to convict them, producing belief, and for churches to be planted among them (II Corinthians 4:3-6 and especially v. 15)?

L. What relationship do you see in Revelation 5:8-14 between the worship and glory brought to the crucified and resurrected Christ and people from every tribe, tongue and nation coming to faith in Him?

> God is a God of missions. He wills missions. He commands missions. He demands missions. He made missions possible through His Son. He made missions actual in sending the Holy Spirit. Biblical Christianity and missions are organically interrelated.   —George W. Peters[4]

Reflect on your thoughts about missions to all people groups and the glory of God.

God wants to restore His creation in the face of a hostile, evil empire still in the process of degrading and destroying it. How should we relate to this God and His glory?

Try to memorize Psalm 96:3. Declare his glory among the nations, his marvelous deeds among all peoples.

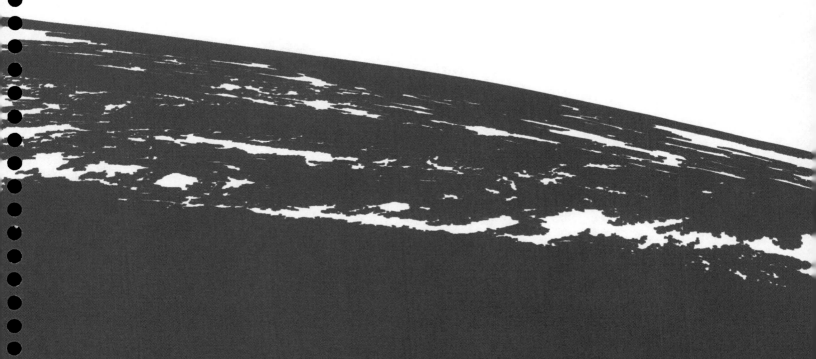

Chapter 2

Faith of Our Fathers—Part 1

2. Faith of Our Fathers-Part 1

God's call of Patriarchs

Missions did not begin after the resurrection through the Great Commission. Let's trace our roots and see how God called some of our spiritual parents in the Old Testament into His service. Wisdom may come from observing the variety of ways God calls people and the variety of missions and ministries in which He calls us to serve Him.

A.   The Call of Abram

    1.   Read Genesis 11:27-12:3. What did God ask Abram to do?

        How difficult a step of faith do you think this was for Abram and why?

    2.   What did God promise Abram?

"They're not going to believe this back home!"

© 1981 Lee Johnson. Used by Permission.

What did God promise He would do through Abram?

3. How do you think all peoples on the earth would eventually be blessed through Abram and his descendants?

The word "nations" seldom means just a country with a political boundary. Many believe "people group" best communicates what is often translated as "nation."

4. What does this teach us about God's covenant and passion from the beginning for all families or people groups to be reached and blessed?

The Great Commission began in the heart of God in eternity past.

5. To what extent can we trust the same God when He calls us to leave our family, homes and home country in His service?

6. Why?

Obedience to God's will is the secret of spiritual knowledge and insight. It is not willingness to know, but willingness to DO (obey) God's will that brings certainty.
—Eric Liddell[5]

B. Moses'Call

Think through how Moses may have felt when God called him to leave his secure environment and go on a dangerous and challenging mission.

1.   What was God's call to Moses (Exodus 3:1-10)?

2.   What do you think Moses may have been thinking about in his first objection (Exodus 3:11)?

3.   What questions do you have about your abilities to serve God through ministry where you live?

4.   What questions do you have about your abilities to serve God through cross-cultural missions?

5.   What was God's response to Moses (Exodus 3:12)?

6.   In God's calling of us today, how trustworthy is this promise?

7.   What parallel New Testament promise and command comes to your mind?
      If in doubt, see Matthew 28:18-20.

8.   What was Moses' second fear (Exodus 3:13)?

9.   Why do you think Moses expected to be asked this question in Egypt?

10.   How did God respond (Exodus 3:14-22)?

11. Based also on John 8:56-59, what does "I AM" mean?

In Scripture, the meaning of one's name can be very significant. God uses different names to reveal His character and plans. For instance, our English texts of Scripture frequently use the word "Lord" for Jehovah (not "Lord," which comes from adoni, meaning master). Sometimes the Hebrew word Jehovah is spelled Yahweh or YHWH. Literally it means, "He is" or "He who is." It is the personal name for God, occurring more frequently than any other name, a total of 5,321 times. Some Biblical scholars understand the meaning of Jehovah to include: He who is truly present, the God who is imminent, the living God of revelation and reconciliation, the personal God of redemption and the covenant-keeping God. All of these traits of Jehovah are in contrast to the homemade idols people have invented as substitutes.

12. Who is the source of our call to mission work?

13. What was Moses' third reservation to God's call (Exodus 4:1)?

14. How would you express that fear today?

15. How did God answer in Exodus 4:2-9?

16. Read I Corinthians 15:3-22. What central New Testament miracle can help an unbeliever listen to who God is?

17. How is this miracle even more significant in showing who God is?

18. State Moses' fourth concern in Exodus 4:10.

19. How do you feel about your ability to learn another language?

20. How do you feel about talking with friends and neighbors about Christ?

21. How do you feel about talking with your friends, pastor and church about missions and your involvement or potential involvement in missions?

22. What is God's response in Exodus 4:11-12?

23. God may want us to talk with unbelievers about Christ, learn another language or talk with believers and churches about missions. When He does, what provision is He able to provide?

24. Why is He able to help us?

25. What was Moses' final response in Exodus 4:13?

26. How would we word this objection today?

27. If God is calling, when is this objection a viable option?

28. What is God's response to "Here am I, send someone else." (Exodus 4:14-17)?

29. How would you describe Moses' personality and character during his call?

30. Reflect on what God may be teaching you from God's call of Moses.

> Sometimes it may be that while we are complaining of the hardness
> of hearts of those we are seeking to benefit, the hardness of our own hearts,
> and our own feeble apprehension of the solemn reality of eternal things, may
> be the true cause of our want of success.
>
> —Hudson Taylor[6]

Try to memorize Genesis 12:2,3 *"I will make you into a great nation and I will bless you; I will make your name great, and you will be a blessing. I will bless those who bless you, and whoever curses you I will curse; and all the peoples on earth will be blessed through you."*

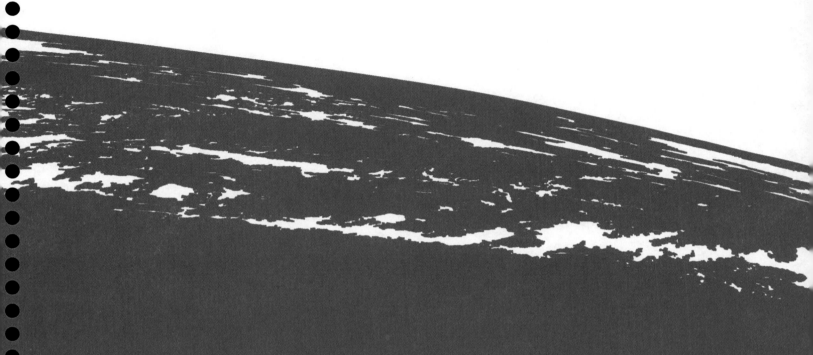

Chapter 3

Faith of Our Fathers—Part 2

3. Faith of our Fathers-Part 2

God's call of statesmen and prophets

God has called individuals throughout the Old Testament by a variety of ways. As you read a few of these ways be thinking of how the same God may be nudging or calling you today.

A. Joshua's Call

   Read Joshua 1:1-9.

   1. What was the circumstance of Joshua's call (Joshua 1:1-2)?

What did God ask Joshua to do (Joshua 1:2-4)?	What did God ask of Joshua (Joshua 1:5-9)?	What did God promise Joshua (Joshua 1:5-9)?

   2. What principles of knowing God's will for your own life do you find in these challenges and promises?

> The motto of every missionary, whether preacher, printer, or school master
> ought to be *"devoted for life."*   —Adoniram Judson[7]

B. Isaiah's Call

1. When and where did Isaiah's call take place (Isaiah 6:1-13)?

2. What was the context of Isaiah's call? On what was Isaiah's call based (Isaiah 6:1-4)?

3. How is the context of Isaiah's call similar to Joshua's call?

4. What was Isaiah's response (Isaiah 6:5)?

5. How did the seraphim respond in Isaiah 6:6-7?

6. What was God's call in Isaiah 6:8?

7. How did Isaiah respond to God's call?

> I thought of all God's people looking out after me with expectation, following me with their wishes and prayers. I thought of the holy angels, some of whom, perhaps, were guarding me on my way; and of God and Christ approving my course and mission. Who will go for me? Here am I, send me.
>
> —Henry Martyn[8]

8.   How much of the details or costs of God's call did Isaiah know?

9.   What lessons do you learn for your own life from God's call and Isaiah's responses?

10. How does Isaiah's response to his call differ from Moses' response to his call?

God's great commission did not begin with Christ's words at the end of His life on earth. For what did God call Israel through the prophet Isaiah in Isaiah 49:6?

> I wasn't God's first choice for what I've done for China. ... I don't know who was. ... It must have been a man ... a well-educated man. I don't know what happened. Perhaps he died. Perhaps he wasn't willing ... And God looked down ... and saw Gladys Aylward ... and God said—'Well, she's *willing*!'
>
> —Gladys Aylward[9]

C.   Jonah's Call

1.   What did God ask Jonah to do (Jonah 1:1,2)?

2.   Where did Jonah head (Jonah 1:3)?

3.   Based on Jonah 1, what may be some of the consequences if we reject God's call today?

4.   If we have first refused to do what God asks us to do, what is a proper response based on Jonah 2:1-10?

5.   What is God's call in Jonah 3:1,2?

"You wouldn't believe what I had for supper."

© 1981 Mary Chambers. Used by Permission.

6. From Jonah 2:10-3:10, how does God respond to repentant people, both nations and prospective missionaries?

7. What does Jonah 4 tell you about Jonah's motivations, ego and attitude?
   What importance does Jonah place on material things, security and his own comfort zone?

> Most Christians would rather be happy than feel the wounds of other peoples' sorrows.   —A.W. Tozer[10]

8. What do we learn about the heart of God for people, especially innocent people, in Jonah 4?

9. What are the motivations, priorities and attitudes of your heart toward people?

   What are your motivations, priorities and attitudes toward material things, security, your schedule and your comfort zone.

10. What do you think God may want you to do about your motivations, priorities and attitudes?

"He is no fool who gives what he cannot keep to gain what he cannot lose."
—Jim Elliot[11]

Try to memorize Joshua 1:8, 9. *Do not let this Book of the Law depart from your mouth; meditate on it day and night, so that you may be careful to do everything written in it. Then you will be prosperous and successful. Have I not commanded you? Be strong and courageous. Do not be terrified; do not be discouraged, for the LORD your God will be with you wherever you go.*

Chapter 4

Christ's View of God's Global Purposes

4. Christ's View of God's Global Purposes?

The Great Commission

We have seen in passages such as Genesis 12:1-3, Psalm 96 and Isaiah 49:6 that God's great commission began long before the end of Christ's life on earth. Christ also taught a lot about missions. His most famous words about missions can be found in what is called His Great Commission. The risen Christ's call for world evangelism was preceded by His rejection by Israel and His ministry to the Gentiles.

A. Therefore, the five accounts of the Great Commission for missions given by Christ are located at the end of the four Gospels and at the beginning of the Acts of the Apostles. Study these five accounts to observe their components: Matthew 28:17-20; Mark 16:15; Luke 24:45-48; John 20:21; Acts 1:8. (Remember in the New Testament Greek language, "nations," "gentiles" and "people groups" have the same original root, "ethnos," from which we today get "ethnic group".)

1. Fill in this chart with the components of the Great Commission where they are mentioned. (Each passage does not have all of the components.)

	Matthew 28:18-20	Mark 16:15	Luke 24:45-48	John 20:21	Acts 1:8
Commands (Verbs)					
Focus Audiences to reach					
Promises					
Authority or Power					

2. What connection is there between the commands and promises?

3. Write out a commission which combines each of the elements of the five accounts of the Great Commission.

4. In Matthew 28 the central imperative in the original Greek is "make disciples." Who are you presently helping to make a disciple of Jesus Christ?

B. Look at the following categories. Which focus groups do you believe Christ is commanding us to exclusively or primarily reach with the gospel?

☐ easy nations

☐ pro-missionary nations

☐ one's home country

☐ easy life-style nations

☐ politically stable nations

☐ nations whose language you have already studied in school

☐ nations whose languages are taught in the West

☐ nations you have already visited

☐ nations in whose language and/or culture you are more comfortable

☐ nations to which, if you go, believers are more likely to support you

☐ nations where you feel secure

☐ people who will not rip you off

☐ people who will have completely pure motivations when they hear and respond to the gospel

☐ ministries where you might be fulfilled

☐ nations without terrorists

☐ nations where you think you may best use all of your education, skills and gifts

- ☐ responsive nations
- ☐ nations who grant missionary visas
- ☐ pro-Israel nations
- ☐ attractive people
- ☐ economically stable nations
- ☐ kind, nice peoples
- ☐ non-resistant peoples
- ☐ peoples who do not persecute or martyr national believers in Christ
- ☐ peoples who do not persecute or martyr missionaries

Now mark those you believe the church has excelled in reaching.

1. Of what type of nation or people group does Christ command us to make disciples in Matthew 28:19?

2. In what part of the world does Christ command us to go and preach the gospel (Mark 16:15, Luke 24:47)?

3. When Christ said to go to all people groups and make disciples of all peoples, were there still major needs and problems at the home base in Jerusalem?

4. Was Christ's command to reach either the home base or all nations, or was it to reach both the home base and all nations?

C. Read Matthew 9:12-13.

How do you think this text is related to the question concerning
where missionaries, evangelists
and pastors are most needed? Are
they needed most among those
who live where they can readily
hear the gospel or those who live
where they cannot hear the good
news?

"Look at me. I've gone into the ministry!"

© 1990 Erik Johnson. Used by Permission.

1. During Christ's ministry, when were these
    commands given?

2. By this timing, what value did Christ place on the Great Commission?

3. If your father or mother at the very end of their lives, clearly asked you to do something, do you think
    you would remember it and try to accomplish it?

D. Some Christians have rationalized away the responsibility to obey the Great Commission by claiming
    Christ's commission was only for the eleven apostles. At the same time, they accept most of Christ's other
    commands as applicable for today. How can you tell from the Matthew 28:19-20 account that Christ was
    directing this commission to all of His disciples in the future?

1. Consider your own motivations for missions and evangelism. How are you influenced by Christ's com-
    mand to make disciples of all nations or people groups?

2.   What do you think Christ may be telling you through His Great Commission?

> It is conceivable that God might have ordained to preach the gospel directly to man through dreams, visions and revelations. But as a matter of fact he has not done this, but rather has committed the preaching to man, telling them to go and disciple all nations. The responsibility lies squarely on our shoulders.
> —J. Oswald Sanders [13]

Try to memorize Matthew 28:18-20. *Then Jesus came to them and said, "All authority in heaven and on earth has been given to me. Therefore go and make disciples of all nations, baptizing them in the name of the Father and of the Son and of the Holy Spirit, and teaching them to obey everything I have commanded you. And surely I am with you always, to the very end of the age."*

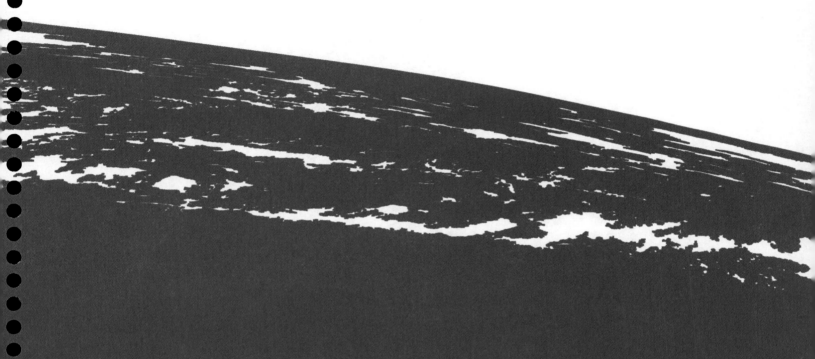

Chapter 5

What Can We Learn from the Early Church?

5. What Can We Learn from the Early Church?

How did the Apostles respond to the Great Commission?

The early church, recorded in Acts and the Epistles, is saturated with motivation and life style examples of missions.

A.   The Love of Christ

Study II Corinthians 5:14-6:2.

What do we learn here about the love of Christ?	What does the love of Christ produce?	What should the love of Christ compel us to do?

B.   Read what John says about love in John 14:15,23,24 and 15:9-17 and in I John 5:3. What is the evidence that we love Christ?

C.   What do you think God may want you to do based on Christ's love?

> But I have given myself up, and I have put myself in the hands of God; and I am resolved to trust in Him as long as I live; I never mean to stop.
> —Amanda Berry Smith[14]

D.   The Joy of God

Read Acts 3:1-10

1.   In Acts 3:1-10 what was the response of the man crippled from birth when a wonderful thing happened to him?

2.   What was the response of the crowd to him?

3.   What might have been your response if you were part of the crowd?

Give an illustration in which you shared a good thing with those who did not have it, rather than keeping it to yourself. What was the other party's response?

4. Based on Acts 3:6-10 what are some advantages of sharing a wonderful thing with those who do not possess it, versus keeping it to ourselves?

5. There are many illustrations in Scripture of people who invested their lives in others over long periods. Think of Moses with Joshua, Eli with Samuel, Christ with His disciples and Barnabas with Mark. Consider the influence of Timothy's grandmother, Lois, his mother, Eunice and Paul in the life of Timothy. What joy do you believe was produced by these relationships?

E. God's Desire

What is God's desire for all people (I Timothy 2:3-6)?

Verse 6 speaks about Christ Jesus "who gave himself a ransom for all." Reflect on the breadth of that statement. How much do you think that motivated Paul? What impact do you think it has on you and your direction and purpose?

F. Paul's Response to the Great Commission.

1. Read Acts 20:17-35. List Paul's actions and attitudes which reflect on his burden to fulfill the Great Commission.

2. Read Romans 1:14-16 and I Corinthians 9:16-23. What do you understand of Paul's passion and method-
    ology for communicating the gospel of Christ?

"Our choice seems
to be between sending
a missionary and
installing new carpet
in the catacombs."

© 1984 Doug Hall. Used by Permission.

3. List some of the contemporary values in our culture such as:

    a. If it feels good, do it.

    b. You deserve a break today.

    c. Look out for number one.

    d. Your goals should be to:
       • be fulfilled.
       • find a job you can love.
       • do your own thing.
       • advance professionally in your career.
       • enjoy the good life.
       • stay within your comfort zone.

    e.

    f.

    g.

    h.

    What do these values teach us?

4. How do these values compare with the effort and price paid by Paul to obey the Lord's command
    (II Corinthians 11:23-33)?

5. What does the Lord say to Paul about the struggle in His life? (See II Corinthians 12:7-9.)

6. Compare your persecutions, problems and challenges, past
    or present, with Paul's.

7. Reflect on how sufficient the grace of God has been in
    your struggles.

Try to memorize II Corinthians 5:14. *For Christ's love compels
us, because we are convinced that one died for all, and therefore
all died.*

> For eighty-six years I have been his servant, and he has never done me wrong:
> How can I blaspheme my king who saved me?
>   —Polycarp, before his martyrdom[15]

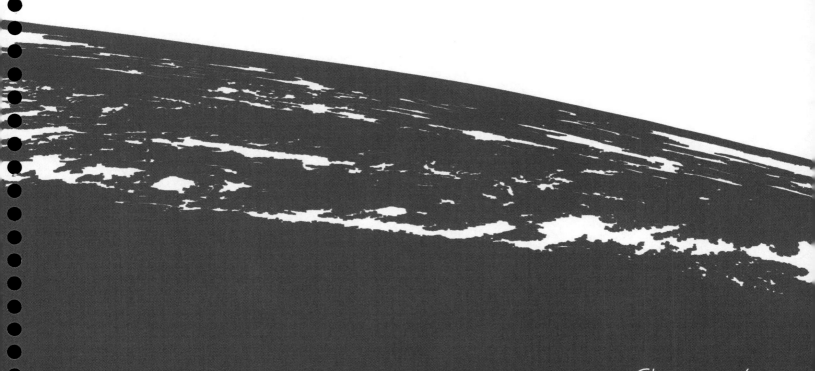

Chapter 6

The King is Coming

6. The King is Coming

How is the Second Coming of Christ related to missions?

The second coming of Christ is one of the strongest motivations for sharing the good news.

A. Christ's Prophecy and Missions

    1. In Matthew 24:14 what is the relationship between preaching the gospel in the whole world and the end of the age? (Remember "nation" can mean "people group.")

    The context of Matthew 24:9 and 21 lead many Bible students to believe that this finally will be fulfilled within the tribulation. Whenever the end of the age happens it is connected to preaching of the gospel in the whole world. Many believe the proclaiming of the good news today around the world precedes Christ's return for the rapture of the church which could occur at any time.

B. Peter's Prophecy and Evangelism

    1. What does Peter say as to why Christ has not yet returned for His second coming (II Peter 3:1-15, especially verses 4 and 9)?

    2. What does Peter say we can do to speed the imminent return of Christ in the light of II Peter 3:9-15, especially verses 9 and 12? (For further study, see Peter's sermon in Acts 3:19-20.)

C.   John's Prophecy and Missions

In Revelation 4 and 5 the 24 elders (who many see as representatives of the church) and the four living creatures worship the lamb, Christ, who is standing in the throne of God. Why do they say He was worthy to open the sealed book (5:9, 10)?

How are God's purposes to be culminated?
See Revelation 5:9-10; 7:9-10.

(Note that the text says believers out of every group of people will praise Christ; it does not say that all will believe.)

© 1993 Doug Hall. Used by Permission.

D.   Reflect on the relationship between the prophecies of Christ, Peter and John. What connections do you see in your own participation with God in missions?

But how does this concept fit together with Christ's promise that He may return at any time (even today) (I Thessalon-ians 5:1-6; Revelation 3:11; 22:7, 12, 20)? One understanding is that Christ may return at any time for the rapture of the Church (I Thessalonians 4:13-18; I Corinthians 15:51-53). Then during the follow-ing seven years of the tribulation, the gospel will spread to all of the remaining people groups. The more people and people groups who become reached with the gospel now, means that fewer will need to be reached for the first time during the tribulation. God's purpose is that in every epoch His good news should go to the whole world.

The world to come at the end of history will be a world without the national barriers that divide people today, a glorious and rich mosaic of peoples, languages, and cultures around the Lamb of God. Missionary internationalization is a clear step in that direction.   —Samuel Escobar[16]

Try to memorize Revelation 5:9,10 *And they sang a new song:"You are worthy to take the scroll and to open its seals, because you were slain, and with your blood you purchased men for God from every tribe and language and people and nation. You have made them to be a kingdom and priests to serve our God, and they will reign on the earth."*

Chapter 7

In 25 Words or Less

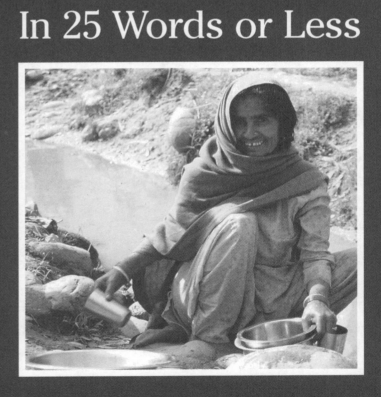

7. In 25 Words or Less

What is essential to the Gospel?

Social work, relief work, economic development, political activism and many other very beneficial things have been substituted for evangelism. These can be very positive and biblical steps for God's glory and man's needs. They can also open doors for the gospel. Matthew 5:16 tells us clearly that we must demonstrate some of the love of God or our words will lose power. Evangelism cannot be separated from the need to demonstrate God's glory. Christ clearly merged the two. But the good can become the enemy of the best if it squeezes out our motivation, resources, time and energy. We do not have energy, finances, time, creativity and resources to do every good thing. If we do things in the order of their importance, we can avoid ending up accomplishing just good things at the expense of the best.

But what is the inner core of the gospel?

A. What was central to the ministry of the Apostle Paul (I Corinthians 1:17-25; 2:2)?

B. How important is it to keep the content of the gospel message clear (Galatians 1:6-12)?

C. What are the components of the gospel as spelled out in John 3:16, 36; Acts 16:31; Romans 1:1-4, and I Corinthians 15:1-8?

D.   Reflecting on your answer in C, in 25 words or less summarize the essential components of the gospel.

E.   There are, of course, significant social and physical ramifications of the gospel. Read Matthew 25:34-46; James 1:27 and James 2:15-18. What social and physical issues mentioned in these passages should concern us?

F.   While preaching the gospel, we also minister in many other ways. What relationship to the Great Commission do you believe the following can have: medicine, education, teaching English as a second language, orphanages, agriculture, economic development, engineering, developing sources of pure water, teaching job skills and the like?

I could not sleep that night ... Within the very touch of my hand were three young girls dying because there was no woman there to help them. ... Early in the morning I heard the "tom-tom" beating in the village and it struck terror in my heart for it was a death message. ... After much thought and prayer, I went to my father and mother ... and told them that I must go home and study medicine, and come back to India to help such women.   —Ida Scudder[17]

G.   Based upon the passages in E above plus Matthew 11:28-30, John 7:37-39 and John 10:10b, how do you think trust in and forgiveness through the crucified and resurrected Christ affect other areas of our lives, such as our brokenness, dysfunctional backgrounds, loneliness, emptiness and physical needs?

© 1981 Joseph Farris. Used by Permission.

Try to memorize John 3:16. *For God so loved the world that he gave his one and only Son, that whoever believes in him shall not perish but have eternal life.*

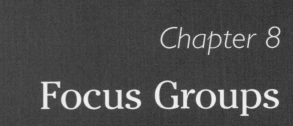

Chapter 8

Focus Groups

8. Focus Groups

Who should be reached with the Gospel?

Messengers of the gospel often develop what could be called a focus group, a specific group of people or a nation, with whom they desire to share the good news. It may be intentional or unintentional, clearly thought out or the path of least resistance.

A. God's Focus

Read Psalm 67.

Below each group jot down the activities related to it, recorded in Psalm 67.

Earth	Nations	Peoples	Ends of the Earth

How many times do you observe these four concepts in Psalm 96?

B. Paul's Focus

Read Romans 15:17-24.

1. What was Paul's personal ambition in Romans 15:20?

2.   How did Paul's ambition affect the spread of the gospel as recorded in Romans 15:19b? (Illyricum included Albania and parts of the Balkans, just east of Italy.)

3.   In what was Paul's faith placed when faced with the question that the unreached might not believe after Paul would go and preach to them (Romans 15:21)?

> There are individuals ripe to receive the Lord in the most resistant and hostile situations. We must take the Gospel to them.   —Virgil Amos[18]

Think through the following passages.

John 15:16 *You did not choose me, but I chose you and appointed you to go and bear fruit—fruit that will last. Then the Father will give you whatever you ask in my name.*

Romans 8:28-30 *And we know that in all things God works for the good of those who love him, who have been called according to his purpose. For those God foreknew he also predestined to be conformed to the likeness of his Son, that he might be the firstborn among many brothers. And those he predestined, he also called; those he called, he also justified; those he justified, he also glorified.*

Ephesians 1:3-14 *Praise be to the God and Father of our LORD Jesus Christ, who has blessed us in the heavenly realms with every spiritual blessing in Christ. For he chose us in him before the creation of the world to be holy and blameless in his sight. In love he predestined us to be adopted as his sons through Jesus Christ, in accordance with his pleasure and will-to the praise of his glorious grace, which he has freely given us in the One he loves. In him we have redemption through his blood, the forgiveness of sins, in accordance with the riches of God's grace that he lavished on us with all wisdom and understanding. And he made known to us the mystery of his will according to his good pleasure, which he purposed in Christ, to be put into effect when the times will have reached their fulfillment-to bring all things in heaven and on earth together under one head, even Christ. In him we were also chosen, having been predestined according to the plan of him who works out everything in conformity with the purpose of his will, in order that we, who were the first to hope in Christ, might be for the praise of his glory. And you also were included in Christ when you heard the word of truth, the gospel of your salvation. Having believed, you were marked in him with a seal, the promised Holy Spirit, who is a deposit guaranteeing our inheritance until the redemption of those who are God's possession-to the praise of his glory.*

II Thessalonians 2:13 *But we ought always to thank God for you, brothers loved by the LORD, because from the beginning God chose you to be saved through the sanctifying work of the Spirit and through belief in the truth.*

God sovereignly has individuals He has chosen to follow Him who will believe when they hear of Christ. God does the choosing, electing, regenerating and placing into the body of Christ. We are His chosen ambassadors, His instruments to bring the great news and finish the job that God has given us. (See II Corinthians 5:20; II Timothy 2:10; I Peter 2:9.)

4. How does Paul describe his focus or passion in II Corinthians 10:15-17?

5. To what extent is Paul's ambition, recorded in Romans 15:20 and II Corinthians 10:15-17, a legitimate and God honoring personal passion and goal for today?

"The question is, How do we win the world to Christ with the minimum of fuss and bother?"

© 1993 Doug Hall. Used by Permission.

Someone has said, "If the church waited until all in Jerusalem were saved and all its social problems were solved before it moved out with the gospel, the church would still exist only in Jerusalem."

C. Our Focus Today

Facts are the fingers of God.   —A. T. Pierson[19]

In John 4:35 our Lord said Do you not say, 'Four months more and then the harvest?' I tell you, open your eyes and look at the fields! They are ripe for harvest.

Christ asked us to open our eyes and look on the harvest field. In the original Greek there are 17 words which we translate "look." Christ chose the word which means carefully contemplate. How can we *care-fully contemplate* the mission fields of the world?

Statistics point out that about 80% of Christian workers minister to the 7.6% of the world population who speak English. Yet many people groups and areas have no workers. About three billion out of six billion people on the earth do not live where they can attend a church to hear the gospel in their language and culture. Ninety-seven percent of the least-reached peoples are in, or come from, the 10/40 Window—from $10°$ to $40°$ latitude above the equator, across Africa and Asia. Most of those who live in, or come from, the Window do not have a reasonable chance of hearing the gospel in their lifetime. Most who live outside of the Window do.

Although there are Christians in every country, of the twelve thousand people groups, six thousand people groups have less than 5% Christian adherents and less than 2% evangelical believers. Key measurements also include the establishment of reproducing churches in each culture.

Based upon passages you have studied like Psalm 96; Matthew 28:19,20; Romans 15:20,21 and Revelation 5:9, a number of followers of Christ are interested in bringing the gospel and planting churches among those least-reached with the gospel.

The least-reached are people who do not have access to a church where the gospel is preached in their own language and culture.

The following charts can help us to more carefully contemplate the open world map. Study the graphic charts of the least-reached blocs of people and those ministering to them on the next pages. Then record who you think are the peoples of greatest need.

What do you think causes this immense imbalance?

To know the will of God we need an open Bible and an open map.
—Attributed to William Carey

More than 95% of the graduates of most U.S. and Canadian colleges and seminaries minister to the 5% of the world who live in the U.S. and Canada.

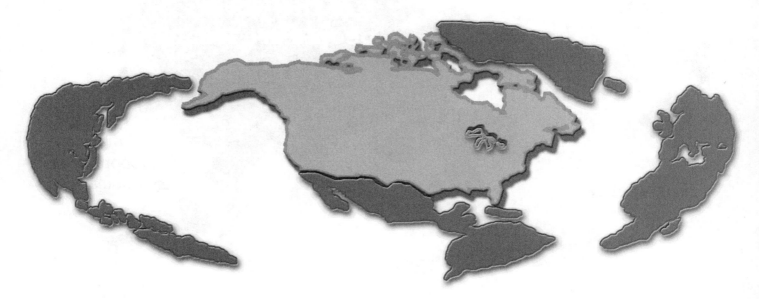

World map drawn in proportion to the opportunity for the world to hear the Gospel through college and seminary graduates from the U.S. and Canada.

The U.S. and Canada have 575,000 churches or one church for every 537 people.

See the introduction for the primary sources of most statistics.

We live in an Asian World

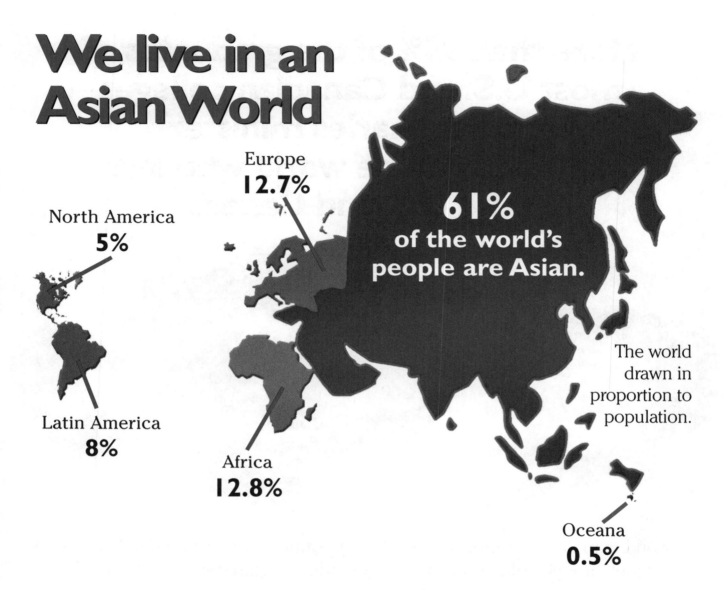

Europe
12.7%

North America
5%

Latin America
8%

Africa
12.8%

61%
of the world's
people are Asian.

The world
drawn in
proportion to
population.

Oceana
0.5%

Asia is the only continent where Christianity is not the largest religion.

Asia is our greatest challenge for world missions.

99% of the unevangelized live outside of the U.S. and Canada.

91% of foreign missionaries minister to professing Christians, not the least-reached.

Four Religious Blocs and the 10/40 Window

Countries with a majority who are Buddhist, Hindu, Muslim or Nonreligious

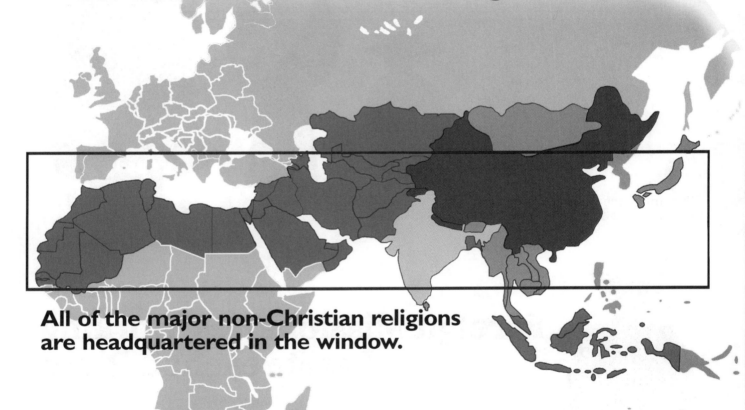

All of the major non-Christian religions are headquartered in the window.

- Buddhist
- Hindu
- Muslim
- Nonreligious

World Total of 56 Countries
44 Muslim countries = 1.27 Billion
2 Hindu countries = 841 Million
8 Buddhist countries = 376 Million
2 Nonreligious countries = 1.3 billion

Least-reached Blocs

Western 100 million	Tribal/Animist 242,882,000	Buddhist 376,574,000	Chinese 400,600,000	Hindu 841,078,000	Muslim 1,271,884,000

Foreign Missionaries Working in Least-reached Blocs

Western 60,000	Tribal/Animist 11,200	Muslim 7,000	Hindu 5,000	Chinese 2,000	Buddhist 1,800

There are 1,299,872,000 Chinese in China, but only about 91,000,000 Christians. Chinese have a variety of religious backgrounds.

Careful Contemplation of the fields
Major Blocs of Peoples outside of Christ

Muslims	**1,271,884,000**
Athiests/non-religious	**924,364,000**
Hindus	**841,078,000**
Chinese (folk religionists)	**400,600,000**
Buddhists	**376,574,000**
Tribal/Animists	**242,882,000**
Total of most non-Christians	**4,057,382,000**
Total Population	**6,364,317,000**

(China's 1,299,872,000 people are primarily atheist/non-religious, folk religionists, Buddhists and Muslims.)

These are mid-2004 statistics.

Number of Foreign Missionaries per Million reaching the Major Blocs

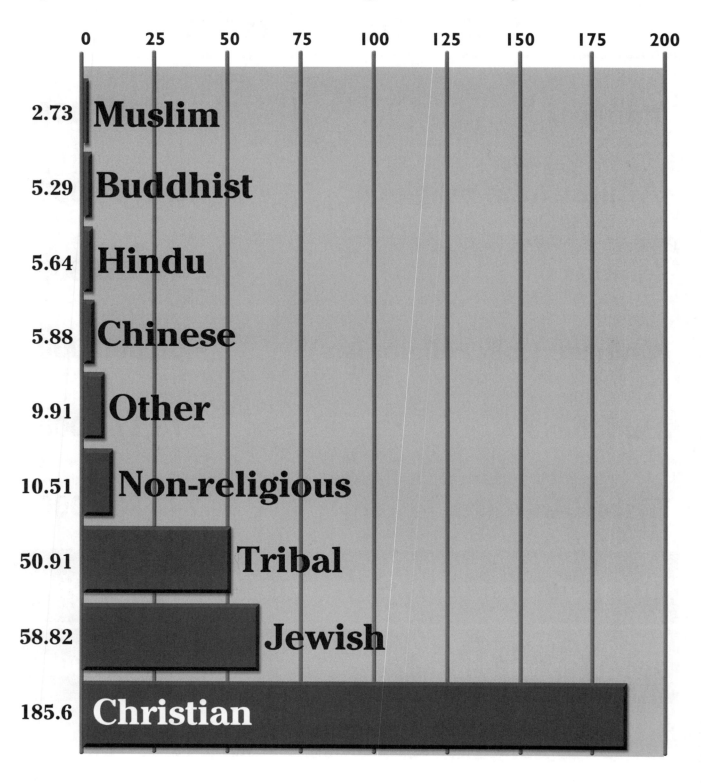

Percentage Distribution of Protestant Missionaries Among Major Blocs

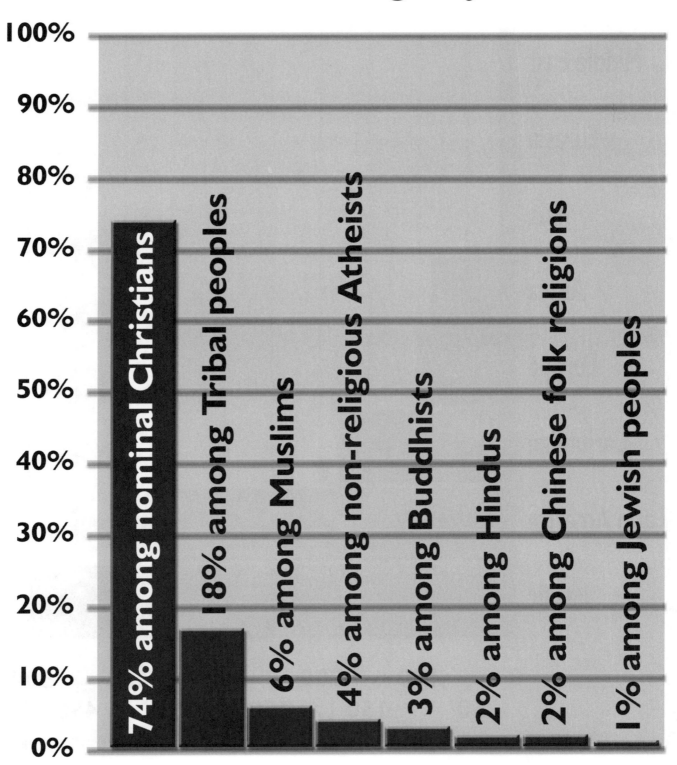

Missionaries Per Million in Geographical Areas

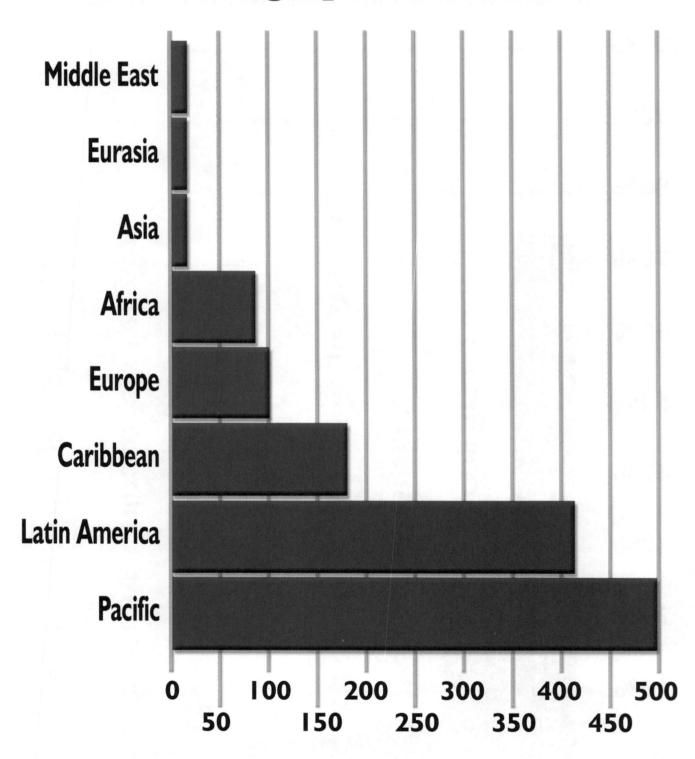

In deciding our place of ministry for Jesus Christ, how seriously should we consider the needs of the whole world or the lack of opportunity of most of the world to hear the gospel?

When we consider needs, what priority should we give to the needs where we currently live that we can see, versus the needs of another region or the whole world?

In determining the will of God for our lives, what part should other peoples' needs play?

To whom do you believe God may be calling you to bring the good news of eternal life in Jesus Christ?

> How do Christians discharge this trust committed to them? They let three-fourths of the world sleep the sleep of death, ignorant of the simple truth that a Savior died for them. Content if they can be useful in the little circle of their acquaintances, they quietly sit and see whole nations perish for the lack of knowledge.
>
> —Attributed to Adoniram Judson

Try to memorize Romans 15:20, 21. *It has always been my ambition to preach the gospel where Christ was not known, so that I would not be building on someone else's foundation. Rather, as it is written. "Those who were not told about him will see, and those who have not heard will understand."*

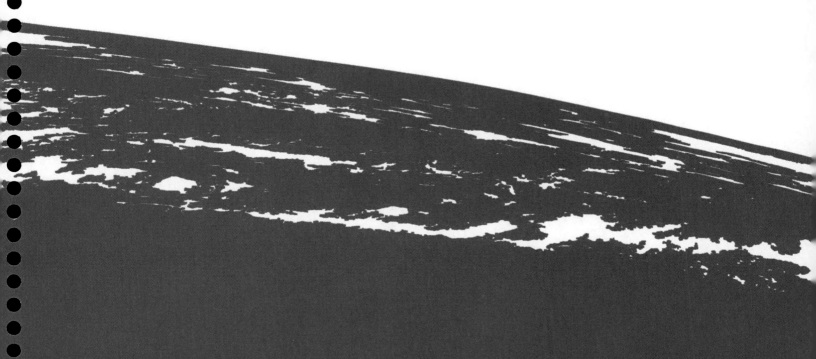

Chapter 9

What about Those Who are Not Reached with the Gospel?

9. What About Those Who Are Not Reached with the Gospel?

Do all roads lead to Heaven?

Our sense of justice can be influenced by our contemporary, biased God-less culture. In the post-modernism of our day, absolutes are a taboo. For many the idea that Christ is the only way of salvation from sin and hell (and the very existence of hell) is "politically incorrect" or absurd. How do you observe the influence of contemporary changing culture and wishful thinking on the theology of our day?

> Behind the shameful apathy and lethargy of the church, that allows one thousand million ... human beings to go to their graves in ignorance of the gospel, there lies a practical doubt, if not denial, of their lost condition.
> —Attributed to A. T. Pierson

In the century since those words were written, the number has escalated to over three billion, but the cause of the church's apathy has not changed. Too often Christians do not really believe that those people who are unevangelized with the good news of Christ are lost.

> The modern habit throughout the Christian church is to play this subject down. Those who still believe in the wrath of God (not all do) say little about it; perhaps they do not think much about it. To an age which has unashamedly sold itself to the gods of greed, pride, sex, and self-will, the church mumbles on about God's kindness, but says virtually nothing about His judgment ... The fact is that the subject of divine wrath has become taboo in modern society, and Christians by and large have accepted the taboo and conditioned themselves never to raise the subject.
> —J. I. Packer[20]

If we believe in heaven because the Bible and Christ taught it, then we have to accept the existence of hell for the same reason. Christ taught more about hell than He did about heaven.

A. The condition of all people throughout history according to Scripture.

1. What is mankind's condition in Isaiah
    64:6 and Romans 3:23?

    Who is included?

    "And this petition requests changing the term 'sinner'
    to 'person who is morally challenged.' "

    What exceptions exist?

    © 1993 Dan Pegoda. Used by Permission.

2. Some believe that everyone has sinned, but the least-reached and heathen are excused because they
    have not yet received a clear understanding of the gospel.

    Read Psalm 19:1-6; Acts 14:17 and Romans 1:18-20. What revelation of Himself has God provided every-
    one (including those who are unreached with the good news of Jesus Christ)? In these passages who
    is the messenger and what is the message that is communicated?

3. What other vehicle of revelation has God provided for everyone according to Romans 2:14-15?

4. What have men done with the light they have received, according to Romans 1:21-25? What examples
    of this today come to your mind?

5. Some acknowledge that the unreached have sinned and have not responded to the light of creation which they have received, yet they do not want to believe that the unreached are completely lost and without hope. What do the following passages clarify about their destiny?

    Psalm 9:17

    Romans 2:12

    II Thessalonians 1:7b-9

    Probably for most of us this is not an enjoyable passage. Truth, however, does not just consist of concepts that make us feel comfortable. We need to be careful not to judge God by our own finite human concepts of fairness and justice. You may want to memorize this passage and meditate on its ramifications.

> *Men are in this plight, not because they are unevangelized, but because they are men.* Sin is the destroyer of the soul and the destruction of the knowledge of God which is life. And it is not the failure to have heard the gospel which makes men sinners. The gospel would save them if they heard it and accepted it, but it is not the ignorance or rejection of the gospel which destroys them, it is the knowledge of sin.
>
> —Robert E. Speer[21]

6. There is truth and error in all religions and many erroneously believe that if an adherent sincerely follows the truth in one's religion, the adherent will find God. Many paths lead up a mountain, so you can take any one as long as you reach the top. Since many paths lead to God, take the one you know and are most comfortable with. How did Christ respond to this thinking in John 14:6, and what did Peter say in Acts 4:12?

> If this view is correct, the logical but unthinkable result will be that Judas and Pilate, Nero and Hitler will eventually fraternize in heaven with Paul and Augustine, Wesley and Moody!   —J. Oswald Sanders[22]

7. What does Paul add in I Timothy 2:3-6 concerning why salvation is found in only one name?

Except for Christ, no significant religious leader has ever claimed to be God, including Moses, Paul, Buddha, Confucius or Mohammed.

8.   What foundational differences exist between biblical Christianity and other religions in regard to the basis of salvation (Romans 10:1-3; Ephesians 2:8-9; Titus 3:4-5)?

9.   Adherents of other religions can do good works and be moral according to their own criteria. According to God's criteria in Isaiah 64:6, what is our self-righteousness or good works like?

Some assume salvation can be gained through good works or a holy life style. How many good works, or what degree of holiness does God require for salvation (I Peter 1:15-16; James 2:10)?

The concept of holiness includes being pure and completely separated from sin. Read Isaiah 53:6; Romans 3:23; Revelation 5:4. What do these passages say about the condition of humans? (Keeping the law for a Jew was essential to being holy.)

10. Some will acknowledge that people who have heard the gospel and rejected it are condemned, but those who have not yet had an opportunity to hear it cannot be condemned. According to John 3:18; 5:24, what is man's status before belief in Christ?

Some believe the unbiblical premise that the least-reached and those who have not really heard who Christ is are not lost. If this belief were true, then evangelists and missionaries would bring condemnation to all of these who hear the gospel for the first time and then reject it. According to this unbiblical premise, it appears it would be better not to tell the unsaved about Christ for fear they may reject Him and become lost. This concept supposes that if we removed every way for the world to hear of God's love in Christ, then everyone would go to heaven. Therefore, if we destroyed or silenced all churches, missionaries, evangelists, Bibles, Christian TV and radio programs, Christian books, literature, schools and hospitals, etc., in one generation, no one would hear the gospel and no one would be condemned and all would go to heaven.

11.   What does I John 5:19 tell about the status of the world?

There is no doctrine I would more willingly remove from Christianity than this if it lay in my power. But it has the full support of Scripture, and especially of our Lord's own words; it has also been held by Christendom; and it has the support of reason. If a game is played, it must be possible to lose it.

If the happiness of a creature lies in self-surrender, no one can make that surrender but himself, and he may refuse. I would pay any price to be able to say truthfully, 'All will be saved.' but my reason retorts, 'without their will, or with it?'
                                                                          —C. S. Lewis[23]

What does Christ teach regarding degrees of judgment or punishment?
See Matthew 11:20-24, Mark 12:40 Luke 12:47,48.

12. What does Revelation 21:8 teach concerning the destiny of unbelievers?

> Would that God would make hell so real to us that we cannot rest; heaven so real that we must have men there; Christ so real that our supreme motive and aim shall be to make the Man of Sorrows, the Man of Joy by the conversion to Him of many ...
>
> —Attributed to J. Hudson Taylor

> It seems to me personally that our failure to have as complete and perfect an understanding of 'fairness' as God does, stems from two things. First, we do not have all the facts. Trying to decide if what He does in a given situation is fair or not, is like coming into a room half way through an argument. Not having all the background information, we are in no real position to cast a verdict. And we won't have all the information until the Judgment Day, when we'll be able to see things in the light of an eternal perspective.
>
> The second reason ... is our own failure to appreciate the seriousness and hideousness of sin. I know that it seldom really strikes me that God owes this utterly rebellious and ungrateful planet absolutely *nothing*. In fact, that is an understatement. Actually He does owe us something—hell.
>
> —Joni Eareckson Tada[24]

13. We who live in the West live in an environment in which diversity and tolerance are two of the highest virtues. They are "politically correct," which in itself is an oxymoron. Our culture carries these two noble virtues to an ignoble extreme. We are taught to be tolerant even of evil, sin and things repulsive to God.

Postmodernism teaches us that "truth cannot be known, everything is relative." (This concept contains a major self-contradiction because the concept itself assumes that it is true and not relative.)

Today's popular theology states that it does not matter what you believe as long as you are sincere. However, suppose in the middle of the night, you were bothered by a cough and you got up to take medicine. If, because it was dark, you took what you sincerely thought was a bottle of cough medicine, but in reality was acid to clean a clogged drain, you would be sincerely wrong. If you sincerely believed a truck was not coming but stepped in front of it, you would be sincerely wrong and sincerely dead. If you got on a plane or bus and sincerely thought it was going toward your home, but it was going in the opposite direction, you would arrive at the wrong destination. There are consequences to being sincerely wrong.

What other illustrations can you think of where sincerity and truth are both important, where it does matter what you believe?

Two opposites can both be false but they cannot both be true. If we say two and two make eight and two and two make twenty-three, they are opposing answers and both are wrong. But two and two make four and two and two make eight are also opposing answers and cannot both be true.

Sloppy, contemporary, popular theology teaches that all religions teach the same thing with no fundamental differences. However, the facts show the opposite. Religions are not variations on a theme, all teaching the same thing. Biblical faith and world religions cannot both be true.

The Bible Teaches:	Some World Religions Teach:	World Religions or Philosophies Which Teach This:
One God	Many gods	Hinduism Animism Ancestor worship
We are to worship only one God, and we are not to make or worship idols.	We are to worship and pray to numerous idols.	Hinduism Buddhism Animism Ancestor worship
It is appointed unto man once to die.	Through reincarnation we can be born and die many times.	Hinduism Buddhism
God and His glory are the ultimate goals of life.	Man and his happiness, fulfillment, development and glory are the ultimate goals of life.	Humanism
Salvation is by grace through faith, not by our works.	Salvation is through our works.	Islam Hinduism Buddhism Animism Ancestor worship
Christ died on the cross for our sins and rose from the dead.	Christ did not die on a cross and did not rise from the dead.	Islam

What do you think that world religions do to the glory that belongs to God alone?

B. How should we respond?

1. As a result of the fear or terror of God, what did Paul do in II Corinthians 5:10-11?

2. Since people apart from Christ are lost, what are some of our responsibilities as Paul outlines them in I Corinthians 9:16; Romans 10:13-17?

> If this indeed is the present condition and future prospect of the heathen—and Scripture seems to offer no alternative—and if the church of Christ has in her charge the message which alone can transform these tragic 'withouts' into the possession of 'the unsearchable riches of Christ,' then how urgent is the missionary enterprise. And how great the tragedy if we fail to proclaim it.   —J. Oswald Sanders[25]

Reflect on what you believe the Word of God teaches about those who are not reached with the gospel.

What do you believe God may want you to do in response?

Try to memorize Acts 4:12. *Salvation is found in no one else, for there is no other name under heaven given to men by which we must be saved.*

Chapter 10

The Sine Qua Non

10. The Sine Qua Non

What is absolutely required to bring the Gospel to all of the world?

Sine qua non is Latin for "without which not"; in other words, "an absolutely indispensable or essential thing." There are some foundational elements in getting out the gospel which are so basic and essential that they can easily be assumed and ignored. However, if they are neglected, it will be a significant detriment to our bringing the great news of the crucified, resurrected and returning Christ to those who are completely without hope and eternal life.

A. The sine qua non of prayer in getting the gospel to every people group:

    1. What is Christ's command in Matthew 9:37-38?

    2. What commitment have you made, or will you make, to pray to the Lord of the harvest for urgently needed workers?

    3. What type of praying does Christ want in Luke 11:5-10 and what does He promise?

    4. What do we learn about prayer in Ephesians 6:18? What kind of praying should we do?

       Give examples from your own prayer life.

5.   In Ephesians 6:19-20, for what did Paul personally ask prayer?

6.   How does this challenge your own prayer life for your growth in outreach to others?

> Satan will always find you something to do when you ought to be occupied about that (prayer and Bible study), if it is only arranging a window blind.
> —J. Hudson Taylor[26]

> The history of missions is the history of answered prayer. ... It is the key to the whole mission problem. All human means are secondary.
> —Attributed to Samuel Zwemer

B.   The sine qua non of mobilizing or recruiting new missionaries to get the gospel to every people group:

We need to consider the process of strategic multiplication for the honor of God. We could lead one person to Christ or recruit ten others who could each lead one person to Christ. We could plant one church or mobilize ten others who could each plant one church. We could reach one least-reached people group with the gospel or discover ten other future missionaries who in turn could reach a least-reached people group with the wonderful news of Christ.

A few are especially gifted in mobilizing, but almost all of us can be used by the Holy Spirit to challenge others to consider their part in helping to get the gospel out to all people groups.

> [We have a] need for 200,000 new missionaries for a new millennium [so that] everyone in the world should receive the gospel and that a church should be planted in every people group.   —George Verwer[27]

1. From Acts 11:25-26a what four actions did Barnabas take in obtaining the new missionary, Saul?

2. Christ recruited and sent out the 12, 70 and 120. Barnabas recruited Saul. On his third missionary journey alone Paul mentions more than 20 disciples who either traveled with him or whom he discipled on the trip. What principles of mobilizing or recruiting future missionaries, do you observe in Scripture?

3. How do you think God could use you to help recruit part of the needed missionary force?

C. The sine qua non of giving and receiving to send the gospel to every people group:

1. Supporting missionaries

    a. What is the significance of sending people for the spread of the gospel in Romans 10:9-15?

    b. What connection do you think exists between giving and sending?

"That was the best sermon on giving I've ever heard."

© 1986 Rob Portlock. Used by Permission.

    c. In Romans 15:24 and III John 5-8 how was giving used in spreading the gospel?

    d. God calls some believers to stay at home, to pray faithfully for missionaries and to work diligently in order to make money, while living conservatively, so they can give generously to send missionaries? Why might this be helpful in reaching all people groups with the gospel?

       What relevance to the above question exists in David's principle recorded in I Samuel 30:24 and the context of verses 21-25?

    e. What would God have you do on a regular basis financially to help send missionaries?

       (If you are discussing your answers you may not want to discuss the specifics of your response to this important question since Christ taught not to let one's left hand know what one's right hand is doing in giving.)

2. Receiving support

Pride and fear prevent some people from getting to the field. They fear they would be perceived as begging and would lose their pride if they became a missionary. Some think if the church, or God's people, supported them it would be like accepting welfare; they would be dependent on society rather than contributing to it. Others fear they might be turned down by churches and, therefore, either do not try or do not keep trying.

    a. In Luke 8:1-3 how did Christ and the disciples receive support?

From this passage what do you learn about accepting financial support from others?

Why do you think Jesus accepted this financial support?

How does that challenge our pride or fear as mentioned above?

b. What does Christ teach about receiving food, shelter and drink from others in Luke 10:5-7?

c. At times Paul lived by the financial support from God's people who sent him and at times he worked with his hands making tents for a living. How did Paul receive income mentioned in Philippians 4:10-19?

(1) In verses 17 and 19 what was the result for those who provided from their resources?

(2) Where is the "account" which holds this credit?

(3) What is the fruit today for those who give to send missionaries with the gospel?

(4) In I Timothy 5:17-18, what did Paul teach concerning financing the teaching and preaching of the Word of God?

3. The Source of our Finances

From Matthew 6:25-34 and 7:11, what does Christ challenge and promise about our finances?

For least-reached people groups to be reached, God uses senders to raise up, strengthen and send missionaries with the gospel. Senders can include: parents, Sunday school teachers, youth leaders, evangelists, pastors, missions committee members, professors, mobilizers, mission board members, mission administrators, financial supporters and prayer partners. Reflect on what part senders contribute.

Study the charts on church spending. What do you believe would be ideal percentages among the four areas of: home church, home missions, regular cross-cultural missions and the least-reached half of the world?

Church Spending

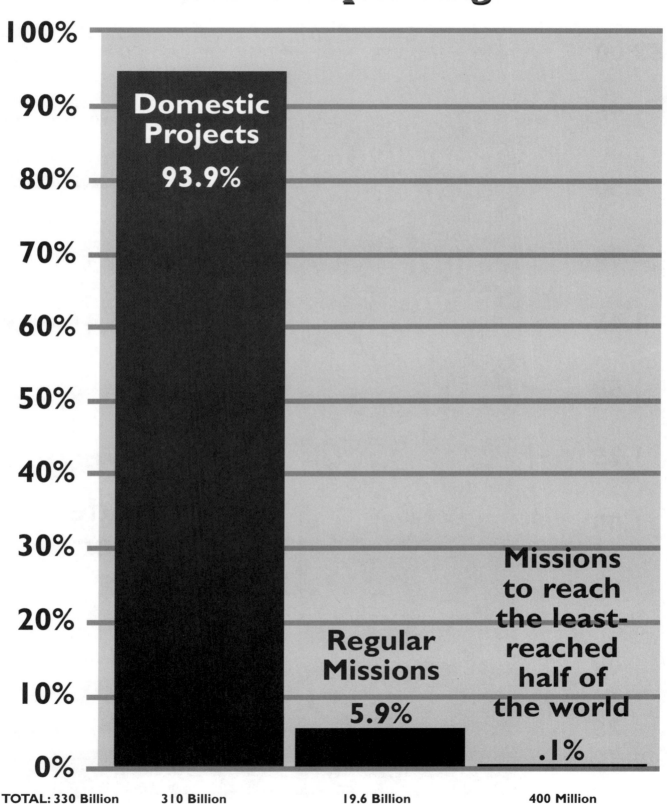

100%
90%
80%
70%
60%
50%
40%
30%
20%
10%
0%

Domestic Projects
93.9%

Regular Missions
5.9%

Missions to reach the least-reached half of the world
.1%

TOTAL: 330 Billion   **310 Billion**   **19.6 Billion**   **400 Million**

Worldwide Giving

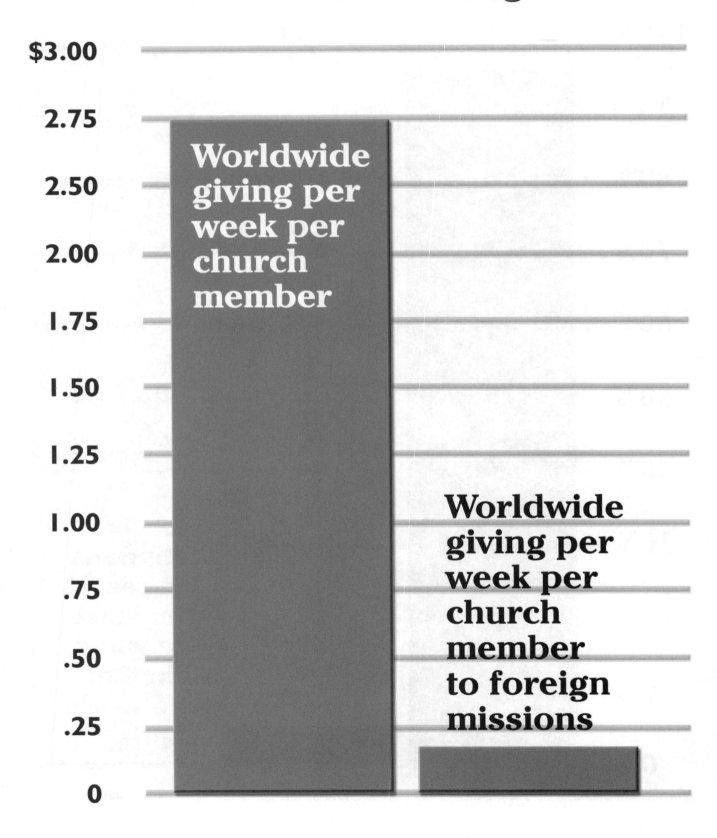

$3.00	
2.75	
2.50	**Worldwide giving per week per church member**
2.00	
1.75	
1.50	
1.25	
1.00	**Worldwide giving per week per church member to foreign missions**
.75	
.50	
.25	
0	

Global Church Member Giving to Foreign Missions

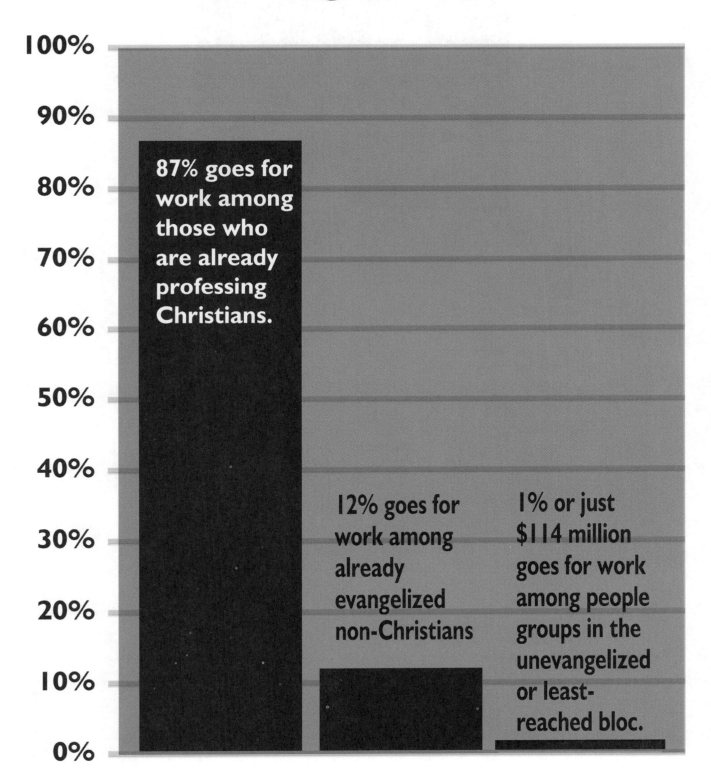

87% goes for work among those who are already professing Christians.

12% goes for work among already evangelized non-Christians

1% or just $114 million goes for work among people groups in the unevangelized or least-reached bloc.

Try to memorize Matthew 6:33 and 9:37-38. *But seek first his kingdom and his righteousness, and all these things will be given to you as well.*

Then he said to his disciples, "The harvest is plentiful but the workers are few. Ask the LORD of the harvest, therefore, to send out workers into his harvest field."

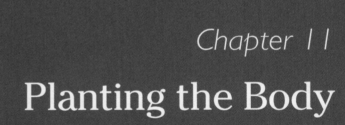

11. Planting the Body

What is the place of church planting in missions?

The Greek word for church, ekklesia, has a root meaning of "called out" and frequently means "called together". The universal church is normally considered to be all believers in heaven and on earth. The local church consists of believers and professing believers in a particular area. There are radical differences between New Testament churches and most Western churches. (The former were household fellowships, not even synagogues.)

In the New Testament and throughout church history, there have been many important methods of missions. It is worthwhile to think through what was central to the New Testament methodology of missions.

A. Christ's attitude toward the church

    1.   Based on Matthew 16:18, what is Christ building now?

    2.   What can destroy the church?

       The word "church" is used only three times in the gospels, Matthew 16:18 and 18:17. Christ is setting up a new structure.

       Satan has control over people who have not heard the gospel. As we go with the gospel where he has control, Satan and the gates of hell will not prevail. As the church is planted where it does not presently exist, it will destroy the grip that Satan has on peoples' hearts and minds. Although individual churches can come and go, the universal church, the body of Christ, will never be defeated by the devil.

    3.   What do you observe that Christ has done for the church in Acts 20:28?

4. What is Christ's position and relationship to the church now as stated in Acts 1:22-23?

5. Why does Christ give spiritual gifts to the church in Ephesians 4:11-12?

6. According to Ephesians 5:25-32, what does Christ do for the church?

7. Summarize your understanding of how Christ values the church.

8. What phrase in these verses expresses Christ's love for the church? What did He do because of this love?

"Don't be alarmed, we're here to plant a church."

© 2000 Jonny Hawkins, Box 188, Sherwood, MI 49089, hawktoons.anthill.com. Used by permission.

9. How do Matthew 16:18; Ephesians 3:10 and Colossians 1:18-24, 25 describe how Christ works through the church?

10. Do you think the church is Christ's central means of working today? Why or why not?

B. Church planting involves expanding the church beyond its borders. The indigenous method of church planting sets as a goal a self-propagating, self-governing and self-financing church.

In the following passages write down what is relevant to planting, nourishing, extending and multiplying the local church?

1. John 21:15-19

2. Acts 2:40-47

3. Acts 11:22-26

4. Acts 13:1-3

5. Acts 14:23-28

6. Acts 15:40-41

7. Acts 19:8-10; 20:17-21

8. I Corinthians 3:5-9

9. Titus 1:5

    Summarize your reflections on the importance and principles of church planting.

C. Wherever the Apostles went they established churches. Why do you
    think this was foundational in the New Testament methodology of
    missions? Why was the comprehensive planting and nourishing of
    the local church their central passion in contrast to just one facet of
    the process, such as only evangelism or only disciple making?

    What place in mission work do you believe church planting should
    have today?

After wrestling with deep doubts about going to the mission
field, Amanda smith said, "But ... to stay here and disobey God—I can't afford
to take the consequence; I would rather go and obey God than to stay here and
know that I disobeyed." Then this hymn came:

> "Lord, obediently I'll go,
> Gladly leaving all below,
> Only Thou my leader be,
> And I still will follow Thee."
> —Amanda Berry Smith[28]

Try to memorize Matthew 16:18: *And I tell you that you are Peter, and on this rock I will build my church, and
the gates of Hades will not overcome it.*

Chapter 12

Yes, But ...

12. Yes, But . . .

Issues and struggles which can side track us from missions.

When considering missions we all have issues, concerns, questions, hang-ups or fears. Some may ask, what if I don't cut it? I may not have the ability to become a quality missionary. I may not be spiritually mature enough or biblically literate enough. Leaving my creature comforts and home culture may be too difficult. It would be too hard for me to leave my family or friends. If I made Cs in Spanish how could I learn Chinese or Arabic? I might not see fruit if I serve Him as a missionary or I might be rejected. I might have health problems or be taken captive or martyred by terrorists. If I have children, there may not be quality education and opportunities for them. My children would miss their friends and grandparents.

Think about your own feelings for a moment. What personal fears, concerns, struggles or barriers inhibit you from witnessing where you presently live, work or study?

What personal fears, concerns, struggles or barriers inhibit you from helping to reach the least-reached?

A. Scripture has a lot to say to our concern that we may not see the fruit we want, or perhaps we will not be able to "succeed" in a ministry or on the mission field.

   What do the following passages teach us about:

   1. The faithfulness of God's Word (Isaiah 55:10-11)?

2. God's promise to those who turn or lead many to righteousness (Daniel 12:3)?

3. In II Corinthians 2:14-17 what does God state or imply regarding different responses to the ministry of the saints?

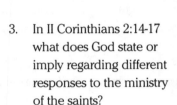

"It's Monty Williams. He wants to know if he can audit your discipleship class on 'Total Commitment.'"

Circumstances may appear to wreck our lives and God's plans, but *God is not helpless among the ruins*. Our broken lives are not lost or useless. God's love is still working. He comes in and takes the calamity and uses it victoriously, working out His wonderful plan of love.

—Eric Liddell[29]

B. Seeing fruit, whether God gives it in this life or in heaven, will take faithfulness on our part. What do the following passages teach us concerning:

1. Our efforts and results (I Corinthians 9:24-27)?

2 Stick-to-itiveness (I Corinthians 15:58)?

3.   Sowing, reaping and becoming weary (Galatians 6:7-10)?

> I can plod; I can persevere in any definite pursuit. To this I owe everything.
> —William Carey[30]

4.   Measurable results versus faithfulness (I Corinthians 4:1,2)?

Some of God's servants may be called to remove rocks from the field and others to plow, plant, water or harvest. But not all harvest. God gives the increase. See I Corinthians 3:5-9.

> Even if I should never see a native converted, God may design by my patience and continuance in the Word to encourage future missionaries.
> —Henry Martyn[31]

Feel free to share your own illustrations of sowing and reaping (evangelism and seeing new belief in Christ.)

C.   Maybe we will face persecution, suffering, discrimination, imprisonment, deportation or martyrdom. What does Scripture say about the possibility of this happening?

John 15:20

Mark 10: 29-31

What promises in the midst of persecution do the following passages provide?

Mark 10: 29-31

> The pioneer missionary, in overcoming obstacles and difficulties, has the privilege not only of knowing Christ and the power of His resurrection, but also something of the fellowship of His suffering.
>
> —Samuel Zwemer[32]

Matthew 5:10,11

Luke 6:22

I Peter 3:13-18; 4:13

> Christ's presence has turned my prison into a blessed heaven. What then will His presence do for me in heaven hereafter?
>
> —Sadhu Sundar Singh from prison[33]

Romans 8:35-39

> I never made a sacrifice. Of this we ought not to talk, when we remember the great sacrifice which *He* made who left His father's throne on high to give Himself for us.   —David Livingstone[34]

How did Christ live out His teaching on suffering and persecution?

> As I wander from village to village, I feel it is no idle fancy that the Master walks beside me and I hear His voice saying gently, 'I am with you always, even until the end.'   —Lottie Moon[35]

6.   Christ's Promises

By way of summary, Christ gave three promises, given first to the missionary though applicable to other Christians. In the light of our desires for family, friends, security, possessions, comfort zones and our own feelings of inadequacy, loneliness, brokenness or lack of ability, what has Christ promised to missionaries in the following passages?

  a. Matthew 28:20

  b. Mark 10:21-31

I had feelings of fear about the future. ... The devil kept on whispering, 'It's all right now, but what about afterwards? You are going to be very lonely'.... And I turned to my God in a kind of desperation and said, 'Lord, what can I do? How can I go on to the end?' And He said, 'None of them that trust in Me shall be desolate.' That word has been with me ever since.   —Amy Carmichael[36]

c. Acts 1:8

Our doubts are traitors and make us lose the good we oft might win by fearing to attempt.
                —Lucio in "Measure for Measure" by William Shakespeare[37]

Reflect on how Shakespeare's statement applies to what we have been studying.

7. Coupled with the promises of God, look at what God has been doing all across the land in answer to prayer:

a. Total foreign missionaries worldwide in 2004 is 439,000.

b. Total fully supported U.S. and Canadian personnel serving overseas (short-term and long-term) from 1992-2001 increased 13.9% to 47,601. (The year 2001 is the most recent date that we have hard figures.)

c. Financial support for overseas ministries raised in the U.S. (adjusted for inflation) from 1992-2001 increased 45.% to $3,752,306,193. This is a growth of 4.5% a year.

d. Financial support for overseas ministries raised in Canada (adjusted for inflation) from 1992-2001 increased by 64.% to $426,585,853. This is a growth of 6.4% a year.

e. The U.S. and Canada have 575,000 churches, or one church for every 537 people.

f. In 1960, evangelicals were 2.8% of the world (84.5 million). In 2000, evangelicals were 6.9% of the world (420 million).

g. Christianity is the most global religion. Christians from Africa, Asia and Latin America, as a percentage of all Christians, have grown from 16.7% to 59.4% between 1900 and 2000. The center of the church numerically and in spiritual power is moving from the North (Europe and North America) to the South (Africa, Asia and Latin America).

h. From 1989-1991 communism collapsed as a global threat, allowing millions of atheists and others to turn to Christ.

i. Today about 94% of the world has access to the New Testament in a language they understand.

j. Each week over 966,000,000 copies of Scripture are distributed.

k. About 50% of the world has viewed the JESUS film. That is three billion people out of six billion.

l. About 99% of the world can view the JESUS film in a language they understand.

m. About 99% of the world has access to Christian radio in a language they understand.

n. In many countries where there is, or has been, severe persecution, the church has grown and strengthened:

Country	1960	2000
Ethiopia	.8% of the population	19.7% of the population
S. Sudan	5% of the population	70% of the population
China	3 million	91 million adherents
India	In 1793 there were few churches	300,000 churches

o. Today India has 44,000 missionaries, of which 60% are working cross culturally

p. In 1884, Korea had its first protestant church; in 2001 South Korea had 31% professing Christians.

q. In 2001 South Korea had 12,000 missionaries: 10,646 are serving in 156 other countries, making Korea the second largest sending country of foreign missionaries.

r. Between 1963 and 2003 more Muslims have come to Christ than ever before in history:
      1979—there were 300 Iranian MBBs (Muslim background believers
      2004—there are about 164,000 Iranian MBBs inside and outside of Iran.

s. Missionaries to Muslims:
      1979—1,000
      2004—7,000+

t. The ratio of unsaved people to Bible-believing Christians in the world:
      In 1793 when William Carey went to India it was-49 to 1.
      In 2004- it is 9 to 1.

u. Most of the immigrants in the West come from the least-reached parts of our globe.

v. More people will hear the gospel of Christ today than at any time in the history of the world.

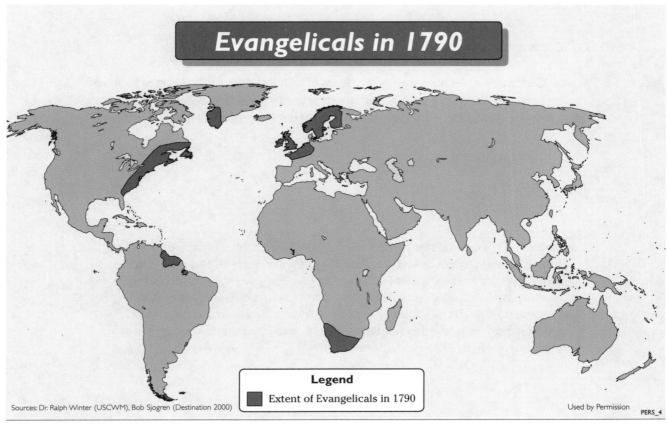

Evangelicals in 1790

Legend

Extent of Evangelicals in 1790

Sources: Dr. Ralph Winter (USCWM), Bob Sjogren (Destination 2000)   Used by Permission   PERS_4

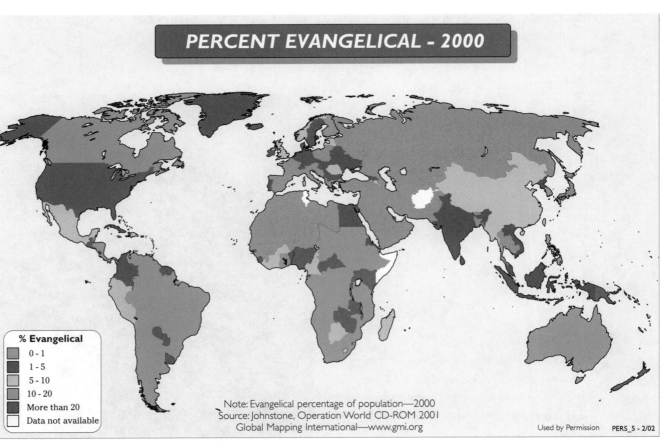

PERCENT EVANGELICAL - 2000

% Evangelical
- 0 - 1
- 1 - 5
- 5 - 10
- 10 - 20
- More than 20
- Data not available

Note: Evangelical percentage of population—2000
Source: Johnstone, Operation World CD-ROM 2001
Global Mapping International—www.gmi.org   Used by Permission   PERS_5 - 2/02

8.   What is my response?

    A. God usually does not ask us to take leaps of faith, just steps, trusting Him in increments. One of the basic questions we need to ask is: How trustworthy is the God of creation and salvation? To what degree do you think you can trust the God of the Bible to fulfill His promises?

> I had utterly abandoned myself to Him. ... Could any choice be as wonderful as His will? Could any place be safer than the center of His will? Did not He assure me by His very Presence that His thoughts towards us are good, and not evil? Death to my own plans and desires was almost deliriously delightful. Everything was laid at His nail-scarred feet, life or death, health or illness, appreciation by others or misunderstanding, success or failure as measured by human standards. Only He Himself mattered.   —V Raymond Edman[38]

    B. Give an experience in your life when you prayerfully took a step or steps of faith and can now look back and see that He was faithful.

Try to memorize Acts 1:8. *But you will receive power when the Holy Spirit comes on you; and you will be my witnesses in Jerusalem, and in all Judea and Samaria, and to the ends of the earth.*

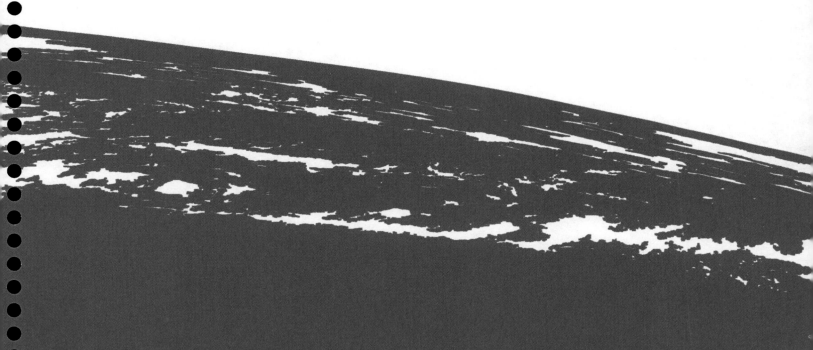

Chapter 13

Here Am I

13. Here Am I

What part should I play?

We have seen how God's passion for missions permeates all sections of Scripture-the Pentateuch, History, Poetry, Prophets, Gospels, Acts, Epistles and Revelation. It is not an afterthought, as some might think, added as an appendix to Christ's ministry. A driving purpose of all of the Word of God is that He be glorified by all peoples. God can accomplish this passion without humans, but He has chosen to call us into His wonderful passion. He gives us the choice of watching from the grandstands or playing with Him on the field.

A.   Notice how the Lord, Christ and Paul observed man's actions or situation and were touched by emotion. Observe what actions result.

    1.   What motive moved God to send Moses to Egypt (Exodus 3:7-10)?

    2.   What was God's emotion which motivated Him to spare the great city of Nineveh in Jonah 3:10, 4:10-11?

3.   What motivated Christ's service in Matthew 14:14?

4.   What motivated Paul in Acts 17:16, 17?

5.   When you see needs around you and around the globe, what is your response?

6.   When you see needs around you and around the globe, what would you like your response to be?

> Let my heart be broken with the things that break the heart of God.
>
> —Bob Pierce[39]

> I believe that (in) *each generation* God has 'called' enough men and women to evangelize all the yet unreached tribes of the earth. ... Everywhere I go, I constantly meet with men and women who say to me, 'When I was young I wanted to be a missionary, but I got married instead.' Or, 'My parents dissuaded me,' or some such thing. No, it is not God who does not call. It is *man* who will not respond!
>
> —Isobel Kuhn[40]

B.   The Completed Church

1.   Based on Revelation 5:9-10, what will be the composition of the Church? (Notice the text does not say "all will believe," but believers will come from "out of" each group.)

2.   What does that tell us about the least-reached 3 billion?

3.   Many believe there are individuals within the thousands of least-reached people groups waiting to be told the gospel, who will believe when we, or someone else, goes and tells them the good news. What a privilege that is! What do you think God may want you to do about it?

> ... we realize that it is not the call of needy thousands. Rather it is the simple intimation of the prophetic word that there shall be some from every tribe in His presence in the last day and in our hearts we feel that it is pleasing to Him that we should interest ourselves in making an opening into the Auca prison for Christ.
> —Nate Saint[41]

> If Jesus Christ be God and died for me, then no sacrifice can be too great for me to make for Him.
> —C. T. Studd[42]

C.   Wisdom for Knowing the Will of God

1.   There are several principles for knowing the will of God, including actively listening to the Word of God, praying and receiving counsel from godly pastors or mentors and from the Holy Spirit. What is the special principle that Psalm 90 (and especially verse 12) teaches for acquiring wisdom to know God's will for our lives?

2.   How many years or days might you have left to help bring the good news of Christ to the nations?

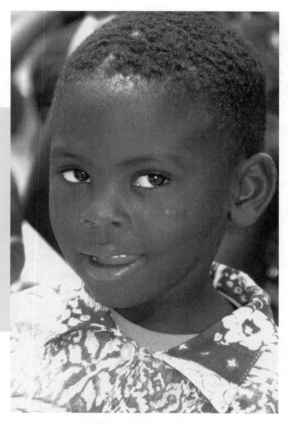

Every man gives his life for what he believes;
every woman gives her life for what she
believes. Sometimes people believe in little or
nothing. One life is all we have, and we live it,
and thus it's gone. But to surrender what you
are and live without belief is more terrible than
dying, even more terrible than dying young. But
there is a worse fate than living without belief. It
is to live with a firm commitment to that which
at the end of life, at the portals of eternity, turns
out to have betrayed you.
                              —Attributed to Joan of Arc

In the light of your always declining number of days, at the threshold of eternity, when you look back
over your life, for what do you want to have exchanged your life? What specifically do you want to try
to become and to get done? What do you believe God wants you to try to be and to accomplish as a
result of your life on this earth?

Are your goals more related to human success or eternal significance?

On earth we all exchange or give our lives for various purposes. Are you exchanging or giving your life for something someone else would have accomplished if you did not do it?

One hundred years after you die, what difference do you hope your life will have made?

There is very little difference between men, but that little difference makes a very big difference.   —Howard W. Ferrin[43]

The value of life is computed not by its duration but by its donation.
                                                        —Attributed to William James

Three things are eternal: God, the Word of God, and the souls of men. Read II Peter 3:10-13. Peter says this world will be burned up. Reflect on Peter's question, What kind of people ought you to be? What results do you want to come from your life on earth, the acquisition of temporal things, caring for the mechanics of living, feeling self-fulfilled or the salvation and nurture of eternal souls?

I would rather die now than to live a life of oblivious ease in so sick a world.
                                                        —Nate Saint[44]

As long as I see anything to be done for God, life is worth having; but O how vain and unworthy it is to live for any lower end!
                                                        —David Brainerd[45]

What primary values and passions for your life do you believe God wants you to have?

**Expect great things from God. Attempt great
things for God**, was the title of a sermon preached by William Carey in 1792
which helped to begin the modern missionary movement.[46]

D.   My Responses

> It is to be kept in mind that the 'generations of men do not wait for the convenience of the church in respect to their evangelization.' Men are born and die whether or not Christians are ready to give them the gospel. And hence, if the church of any generation does not evangelize the heathen of that generation, those heathen will never be evangelized at all.
>
> It is always true in the work of evangelization that the present can never anticipate the future, and that the future can never replace the past. What is to be done in soul saving must be done by that generation.
>
> —J. Oswald Sanders[47]

1. According to II Corinthians 6:2 and II Timothy 4:2, when is the best time for evangelism and ministering?

> This is a decision we do not make, because it has already been made. Whether we spend our lives for the purpose of reaching all men with the gospel is not optional. Christ has commanded every Christian to do just this. Now there are many different ways of accomplishing this one purpose—but regardless of the particular work God has for each of us to do, the one aim of us all in doing our particular job for the Lord must be the evangelization of the whole world.
> —Attributed to G. Allen Fleece

2. What work do you think God may have for you in His purpose of the evangelization of the whole world?

Try to memorize Isaiah 6:8. *Then I heard the voice of the LORD saying, Whom shall I send? And who will go for us? And I said, Here am I. Send me!*

Chapter 14

Putting It All Together

14. Putting It All Together

A summary of my study and prayer

Now take the time to read over your observations and applications written in this study, and be thinking how you will answer the following four questions. You may want to highlight some of your notes.

1. If you were asked to teach a series of five lessons on missions, what five texts would you choose, and what would be the central idea of each message?

    a.

    b.

    c.

    d.

    e.

2. Based upon your study of Scripture, your walk with the Lord and prayer, what are your central motivations and biblical foundations for your own missionary effort?

3. How do you think God is nudging you? What goals do you believe God may want you to have for your life?

> ... if God has called you to China or any other place and you are sure in your own heart, let nothing deter you. ... remember it is God who has called you and it is the same as when He called Moses or Samuel.
>
> —Gladys Aylward[48]

4. What specific things would you like to change in your life based upon your prayer, your observations of all the passages in this study and God's feedback from the process?

> Tell the students to give up their small ambitions and come eastward to preach the gospel of Christ ...   —Francis Xavier[49]

> There are individuals ripe to receive the Lord in the most resistant and hostile situations. We must take the Gospel to them.   —Virgil Amos[50]

Recommended passages to memorize:

Chapter 1 Psalm 96:3 *Declare his glory among the nations, his marvelous deeds among all peoples.*

Chapter 2 Genesis 12:2,3 *I will make you into a great nation and I will bless you; I will make your name great, and you will be a blessing. I will bless those who bless you, and whoever curses you I will curse; and all peoples on earth will be blessed through you.*

Chapter 3 Joshua 1:8,9 *Do not let this Book of the Law depart from your mouth; meditate on it day and night, so that you may be careful to do everything written in it. Then you will be prosperous and successful. Have I not commanded you? Be strong and courageous. Do not be terrified; do not be discouraged, for the LORD your God will be with you wherever you go.*

Chapter 4 Matthew 28:18-20 *Then Jesus came to them and said, "All authority in heaven and on earth has been given to me. Therefore go and make disciples of all nations, baptizing them in the name of the Father and of the Son and of the Holy Spirit, and teaching them to obey everything I have commanded you. And surely I am with you always, to the very end of the age."*

Chapter 5 II Corinthians 5:14 *For Christ's love compels us, because we are convinced that one died for all, and therefore all died.*

Chapter 6 Revelation 5:9,10 *And they sang a new song: "You are worthy to take the scroll and to open its seals, because you were slain, and with your blood you purchased men for God from every tribe and language and people and nation. You have made them to be a kingdom and priests to serve our God, and they will reign on the earth."*

Chapter 7 John 3:16 *For God so loved the world that he gave his one and only Son, that whoever believes in him shall not perish but have eternal life.*

Chapter 8 Romans 15:20,21 *It has always been my ambition to preach the gospel where Christ was not known, so that I would not be building on someone else's foundation. Rather, as it is written: "Those who were not told about him will see, and those who have not heard will understand."*

Chapter 9 Acts 4:12 *Salvation is found in no one else, for there is no other name under heaven given to men by which we must be saved.*

Chapter 10 Matthew 6:33 and 9:37-38 *But seek first his kingdom and his righteousness, and all these things will be given to you as well.*

Then he said to his disciples, "The harvest is plentiful but the workers are few. Ask the LORD of the harvest, therefore, to send out workers into his harvest field."

Chapter 11 Matthew 16:18 *And I tell you that you are Peter, and on this rock I will build my church, and the gates of Hades will not overcome it.*

Chapter 12 Acts 1:8 *But you will receive power when the Holy Spirit comes on you; and you will be my witnesses in Jerusalem, and in all Judea and Samaria, and to the ends of the earth.*

Chapter 13 Isaiah 6:8 *Then I heard the voice of the LORD saying, "Whom shall I send? And who will go for us?" And I said, "Here am I. Send me!"*

Quotation Sources

1. From a speech by Henry Ford.

2. John Piper, *Let the Nations Be Glad!: The Supremacy of God in Missions* (Grand Rapids: Baker Books, 1993), p. 11.

3. John Piper, *Let the Nations Be Glad!: The Supremacy of God in Missions* (Grand Rapids: Baker Books, 1993), p. 15.

4. George W. Peters, *A Biblical Theology of Missions* (Chicago: Moody Press, 1972), p. 346.

5. Eric Liddell, *The Disciplines of the Christian Life* (Nashville: Abingdon Press, 1985), p. 165.

6. Hudson Taylor, *Hudson Taylor's Choice Sayings: A Compilation from His Writings and Addresses* (London: Morgan & Scott, Ltd.: ND), p. 73.

7. Courtney Anderson, *To the Golden Shore: The Life of Adoniram Judson* (New York: Little Brown and Company, 1956), p. 409.

8. A. Thomson, *Great Missionaries: A Series of Biographies* (New York: T. Nelson & Sons, 1862), p. 245.

9. Phyllis Thompson, *The Transparent Woman* (Grand Rapids: Zondervan Publishing House, 1971), pp. 182-183.

10. J. Oswald Sanders, *What of Those Who Have Never Heard* (Crowborough, East Sussex: Highland Books, 1986) p. 139.

11. Elizabeth Elliot, *Shadow of the Almighty: The Life and Testament of Jim Elliot* (New York: Harper & Row, 1958), p. 15.

12. J. Oswald Sanders, *What of the Unevangelized?* (London: Overseas Missionary Fellowship, 1967), p. 71.

13. Amanda Smith, *An Autobiography: The Story of the Lord's Dealings with Mrs. Amanda Smith, the Colored Evangelist* (New York: Garland Publishing, Inc., 1987), p. 359.

14. Eusebius, *History of the Church in Eerdman's Handbook to the History of Christianity* (Grand Rapids: Eerdmans, 1977), p. 81.

15. Samuel Escobar, *The Internationalization of Missions and Leadership Style* (Speech to the 1991 Evangelical Foreign Mission Association annual convention).

16. Mary Pauline, *Dr. Ida: India: The Life-Story of Ida S. Scudder* (New York: Fleming H. Revell Company, 1938), p. 51.

17. Jean Voss Sorokin, "Virgil Amos" in *African-American Experience in World Mission: A Call Beyond Community*, Vaughn J. Walston and Robert J. Stevens, ed. (Pasadena: William Carey Library, 2002), p. 71.

18. A. T. Pierson, *Missionary Review of the World*, 1888.

19. James I. Packer, "*The Wrath of God,*" The Evangelical Magazine.

20. Robert E. Speer, "*Are the Unevangelized Heathen Lost?,*" Sunday School Times.

21. J. Oswald Sanders, *What of Those Who Have Never Heard?* (Crowborough, East Sussex: Highland Books), p. 11.

22. C. S. Lewis, *The Problem of Pain* (London: C. Bles, 1940), p. 106.

23. Joni Eareckson, *A Step Further* (Glasgow: Pickering & Inglis), p. 170.

24. J. Oswald Sanders, *What of Those Who Have Never Heard?* (Crowborough, East Sussex: Highland Books, 1986), p. 104.

25. Dr. & Mrs. Howard Taylor, *Hudson Taylor's Spiritual Secret* (Chicago: Moody Press, n.d.), p. 235.

26. George Verwer, *Out of the Comfort Zone* (Minneapolis: Bethany House, 2000), p. 121.

27. Amanda Smith, *An Autobiography: The Story of the Lord's Dealings with Mrs. Amanda Smith, The Colored Evangelist* (New York: Garland Publishing, Inc. 1987), p. 246.

28. Eric Liddell, *The Disciplines of the Christian Life* (Nashville: Abingdon Press, 1985), p. 125.

29. A. Thomson, *Great Missionaries: A Series of Biographies* (New York: T. Nelson & Sons, 1862), p. 225.

30. Samuel M. Zwemer, *Islam: A Challenge to Faith* (New York: Student Volunteer Movement for Foreign Missions, 1909), p. 197.

31. David and Naomi Shibley , *The Smoke of a Thousand Villages... and Other Stories of Real Life Heroes of the Faith* (Nashville: Thomas Nelson Publishers, 1989), p. 122.

32. Eugene Myers Harrison, *Missionary Crusaders for Christ* (by the author, 1967), p. 54.

33. J. H. Worcester, Jr., *David Livingstone* (Chicago: Moody Press, 1987), p. 57.

34. Catherine B. Allen, *The New Lottie Moon Story* (Nashville: Broadman Press, 1980), p. 132.

35. Frank Houghton, *Amy Carmichael of Dohnavur: The Story of a Lover and Her Beloved* (Fort Washington, PA: Christian Literature Crusade, 1953), p. 62.

36. William Shakespeare, *Measure for Measure,* Act 1, Scene 4, lines 78-79.

37. V. Raymond Edman, *They Found the Secret* (Grand Rapids: Zondervan Publishing House, 1960), p. 150.

38. W. Dayton Roberts, "Robert (Bob) Willard Pierce," in *Biographical Dictionary of Christian Missions,* ed. Gerald Anderson (New York: Simon & Schuster MacMillan, 1998), p. 535.

39. Isobel Kuhn, *Nests Above the Abyss* (Singapore: Overseas Missionary Fellowship, 1947), p. 224.

40. Russell T. Hitt, *Jungle Pilot: The Life and Witness of Nate Saint* (New York: Harper & Brothers, 1959), p. 288.

41. Norman Grubb, *Christ in Congo Forests: The Story of the Heart of Africa Mission* (London: Lutterworth Press, 1945), p. 13.

42. Richard Seume, *Shoes for the Road* (Chicago: Moody Press, 1975), p. 7.

43. Bobert Savage, *At Your Orders, Lord!* (Grand Rapids: Zondervan, 1957), p. 45.

44. Jonathan Edwards, *The Life of David Brainerd, Missionary to the Indians* (New York: The Christian Alliance Publishing Company, 1925), p. 190.

45. Basil Miller, *William Carey: The Father of Modern Missions* (Minneapolis: Bethany House Publishers, 1980), p. 37.

46. J. Oswald Sanders, *What of Those Who Have Never Heard* (Crowborough, East Sussex: Highland Books, 1966), p. 134.

47. Phyllis Thompson, *The Transparent Woman* (Grand Rapids: Zondervan Publishing House, 1971), p. 51.

48. C. S. Lewis, *The Weight of Glory and Other Addresses*, Revised and Expanded Edition (New York: MacMillan, 1980), pp. 18-19.

49. Michael C. Griffiths, *Give Up Your Small Ambitions* (Chicago: Moody Press, 1979), p. 4.

50. Jean Voss Sorokin "Virgil Amos" in *African-American Experience in World Mission: A Call Beyond Community*, Vaughn, J. Wolston and Robert J. Stevens, ed. Pasadena: William Carey Library, 2002), p. 71.

Biographical Sketches

Virgil Amos (1942-   ) served ten years with Operation Mobilization in Asia. He is the founder and General Director of Ambassadors Fellowship, a mission designed to help minorities get to the field.

Gladys Aylward (1902-1970), from England, was made famous by the movie "The Inn of the Sixth Happiness," starring Ingrid Bergman. A reputable mission turned her down because they thought she was not missionary material and lacked academic ability, yet she became the most well known single woman missionary. While fleeing the Japanese in China, she led 100 orphaned children 240 miles to safety.

David Brainerd (1718-1747) served with The Scottish Society for the Propagation of Christian Knowledge as a missionary among Native Americans. He usually served alone among the Mohicans in Massachusetts and Delawares in Pennsylvania and New Jersey. His diaries were edited by Jonathan Edwards, whose daughter Jerusha Edwards, was engaged to Brainerd at the time of Brainerd's death at age 29 from tuberculosis. Brainerd's journals, published after his death, show the hardships of ministry in the wilderness, revivals among Native Americans as well as Brainerd's melancholy personality, ill health and deep dependence upon God. Hundreds of missionaries have received part of their call to missions through reading his journals, including Henry Martyn and William Carey.

William Carey (1761-1834) is known as the father of modern missions. A shoemaker from age 16 to 28 in England, he made a map of the world and put it over his cobbler's bench to remind him of the world's needs and to pray for them. He helped to form the Baptist Missionary Society and wrote to other denominations encouraging them to do the same, which they did. He served for 40 years in India without a furlough.

Carey supervised and edited the translation of the Bible into 36 languages and founded the Agricultural and Horticultural Society of India and Serampore College. He helped encourage Hindu members of Parliament to outlaw widow burning and infanticide. For many years he was a self-supporting tentmaker as manager of an indigo plantation and later as professor in Calcutta of Hindi languages, including Bengali, Sanskrit and Marathi.

Amy Carmichael (1867-1951) was first turned down as a missionary candidate for health reasons. She served first in Japan and Ceylon and then for 55 years without a furlough in South India, with the Church of England Zenana Missionary Society. She founded the Dohnavur Fellowship which rescued and raised children devoted to temple prostitution throughout India.

Amy came from a wealthy north Ireland family and wrote 35 books. She served her last 20 years as an invalid on the mission field, writing and empowering other leaders.

Victor Raymond Edman (1900-1967) served as a missionary of the Christian and Missionary Alliance five years in Ecuador and from 1940-1965 as President of Wheaton College. He was the author of over 20 books.

Jim Elliot (1927-1956) Plymouth Brethren missionary to Ecuador, was martyred at age 29, along with four friends by the Auca Indians, to whom they were seeking to bring the love of Christ. Their martyrdom has helped produce both many believers among the Auca and thousands of missionaries. He was a champion wrestler, graduated summa cum laude from Wheaton College and attended the first two Urbana missionary conferences.

J. Samuel Escobar (1934-   ) from Peru, serves as President of the United Bible Societies and Professor of Missions at Eastern Baptist Theological Seminary.

Howard W. Ferrin (1898-1993) from 1925 to 1965 served as president of Providence Bible Institute (Barrington College) which merged with Gordon College in 1985. Ferrin led P.B.I. in its greatest growth.

G. Allen Fleece (1909-1996) a Presbyterian minister, served as the second president of Columbia Bible College, now Columbia International University.

Henry Ford (1863-1947) known as the "father of the automobile," helped invent mass production.

William James (1842-1910) taught philosophy and psychology at Harvard and popularized pragmatism.

Joan of Arc (1412-1431) national heroine and second patron of France, was an illiterate, devout peasant girl who unified France. She gathered troops to kick the English out of France and routed them from Orleans, the turning point of the Hundred Years War. Captured by the Burgundians, she was sold to the English, charged with witchcraft and heresy and burned at the stake as a teenager.

Adoniram Judson (1788-1850) helped form the American Board of Commissioners for Foreign Missions, the first foreign mission board out of the United States in 1810. Later, after he became a Baptist, he formed the American Baptist Foreign Mission Society. From 1813-1849 he served in Burma (Myanmar), wrote a dictionary, helped to translate the Burmese Bible and left the legacy of a strong Burmese church. At his death, there were 2,700 missionaries from the mission boards he formed.

Isobel Kuhn (1901-1957), from Canada, served with the China Inland Mission among the Lisu people in China and Thailand. Her eight books and numerous articles were prompted by personal discouragements which she honestly communicated.

C. S. Lewis (1898-1964) novelist, poet, apologist and Angelican layman, taught at both Oxford and Cambridge. He was a prolific writer, averaging about a book a year. Much of his work was intended to remove the objections Christians face in our secular, humanistic, agnostic age. More than 40 million copies of his books are in print, making Lewis the best-selling Christian author in history.

Eric Liddell (1902-1945) is remembered best as the Olympic champion of the Academy Award winning film, Chariots of Fire, but he also grew up as an MK and later served as a missionary with the London Missionary Society. He died in a prisoner of war camp in China, the country of his birth and ministry. Known as the "Flying Scotsman," he refused to run the 100 meter race in the 1924 Olympics, giving up the chance to win a gold medal, because the race took place on a Sunday. He did run in the 400 meter race for which he was not prepared and set a new world record, bringing the Olympic gold home to Great Britain.

David Livingstone (1813-1873) physician, missionary and geographer with the London Missionary Society, traveled more than 30,000 miles over the African continent, much of it on foot with the help and friendship of his national companions. Largely as a result of his reports, slavery became illegal throughout much of the world. His heart was buried where he died in Zambia and the rest of his body lies in Westminster Abbey, in London.

Henry Martyn (1781-1812) Angelican chaplain and missionary to India and Iran, helped translate the New Testament into Urdu, Persian and Arabic before his death at 31. Martyn held a passion for studying and understanding Islam, a non-combative attitude toward Muslims and a respect for Indian culture.

Lottie Moon (1840-1912), from Virginia, served 40 years in Northern China and is considered the patron saint of Southern Baptist Missions. Through her writing from China, she stirred missions in Southern Baptist's hearts which continue to be moved to this day. She has aided the Southern Baptists to become the largest denominational foreign mission board. Each Christmas more than 80 million dollars is collected in the Lottie Moon offering for foreign missions, which she had suggested.

J. I. Packer (1926-   ), evangelical Anglican, was born in Oxford, England, and now serves as Professor of Theology at Regent College in Vancouver, British Columbia. Packard is a prolific writer and Senior Editor of Christianity Today.

George W. Peters (1907-1988), Ukraine-born Professor of Missions at Dallas Theological Seminary (1962-1976), served as Academic Dean of Mennonite Brethren Biblical Seminary and helped establish a mission training center in Germany.

A. T. Pierson (1837-1911), a Presbyterian minister in the US, was editor of the Missionary Review of the World and an original editor of the Scofield Reference Bible. Pierson was a leader in the student volunteer movement who wrote over 50 books and was called the greatest popularizer of missions in his lifetime. Pierson helped found the Student Volunteer Movement and originated the watchword of the SVM "The Evangelization of the World in this Generation." Over 20,000 members of the SVM became missionaries. The mission passion of John R. Mott, Stephen Neill, Robert Speer, Samuel Zwemer and many others is traceable to Pierson's preaching or writing. He helped to found the Africa Inland Mission and functioned as a patriarch to the growing faith mission movement.

Dr. John Piper (1946-   ), a prolific reformed writer, has served since 1980 as Senior Pastor of Bethlehem Baptist Church, an inner city church in Minneapolis, Minnesota.

Polycarp (ca. 69—ca. 156) was a disciple of the apostle John and a last link of the church with the Apostolic age. He served as Bishop of Smyrna (Izmir) before being burned at the stake at age 86. He wrote a letter to the Philippians similar to the Apostle Paul's, encouraging them to strengthen their practical spiritual walk.

Nate Saint (1923-1956) was martyred by the Auca Indians in Ecuador January 8, 1956 along with four teammates. Saint, an MAF pilot, flew gifts and the team to the Aucas.

J. Oswald Sanders (1902-1992), former General Director of the Overseas Missionary Fellowship (formerly China Inland Mission) from New Zealand, pioneered the acceptance of Asians as missionaries. Later Sanders was a world traveling Bible teacher, writing 35 books, 20 of them after the age of 70. They have been translated into more than 20 languages. Previously he was the solicitor of the Supreme Court of New Zealand and has been the principal of a Bible college in New Zealand and New Guinea.

Ida Scudder (1870-1960), MK and MD from India to India, came from a family in which 42 members served as missionaries in four generations, primarily as medical missionaries in India. Ida founded the 484 bed General Hospital in Vellore, one of the largest in all Asia at the time, as well as a 60-bed eye hospital, the first graduate school of nursing in India and numerous mobile clinics. She also trained some 200 medical students per year.

William Shakespeare (1564-1616), a genius with little formal schooling, wrote 38 plays which are read and acted to this day. Shakespeare possessed a unique ability to communicate his insight into human nature through dramatic speech and action. He built universal truths so clearly that they are as applicable to this day as when they were first presented in the Globe Theater in Stratford-on-Avon. After the Bible, Shakespeare is quoted more than any other literary source in the English language.

Sadhu Sundar Singh (1889-1929), a believer in Christ from a mixed Sikh and Hindu background, lived the life of a holy mystic, evangelizing in northern India and Tibet on an annual basis between 1908 and 1929. He suffered continuous persecution and had miraculous deliverances. In 1929 Singh set off for Tibet but was never heard from or seen again.

Amanda Berry Smith (1837-1915) was born into slavery in Maryland and after the death of her youngest child and her husband, she gave herself to missions and evangelism on four continents.

Robert E. Speer (1867-1947) one of the earliest student volunteers, served as secretary of the Presbyterian Board of Foreign Missions for 46 years and authored 67 books. He was a national leader for world missions in the first half of the twentieth century.

C. T. Studd (1860-1931) was considered by many to be England's greatest cricketer and a member of the Cambridge Seven. He went to China under the China Inland Mission for nine years. Leaving his wealth and fame for China, Studd helped spark the growth of the Student Volunteer Movement in England. Later he served in India for six years and then in Africa in the Belgian Congo for 18 years. He began the Heart of Africa Mission which became the foundation of WEC (Worldwide Evangelization Crusade) which today serves in 51 countries with 1,500 missionaries. Unevangelized Fields Missions (UFM) came out of WEC.

Joni Eareckson Tada (1949 -   ) was injured during a diving accident in 1967, which left her as a wheelchair-bound quadriplegic. She learned to paint with a brush between her teeth and began Joni and Friends, an organization to encourage the disabled community. Her radio program, Joni and Friends, is heard over 800 stations. Joni has authored 27 books, including her best-selling autobiography, Joni.

J. Hudson Taylor (1832-1905) founded the China Inland Mission (later the Overseas Missionary Fellowship) which led to the founding of other faith missions. He stressed identification with the Chinese people, such as wearing Chinese dress and hair styles, trusting God alone for financial needs and directing the mission from the field. In 30 years the CIM grew to 825 missionaries, 500 Chinese partners and 25,000 Chinese believers. It became the largest foreign mission organization in the world, peaking in 1934 with 1,368 missionaries. Eventually, the China Inland Mission served over 6,000 missionaries from different boards, predominantly in the interior of China.

A. W. Tozer (1897-1963) served pastorates in the Christian and Missionary Alliance and functioned as an evangelical prophetic mystic, merging doctrine and devotion. For many years Tozer edited the Alliance Witness, probably reaching more people through his writing than his preaching.

George Verwer (1938 -   ) founded Operation Mobilization which has sent out 120,000 short-term missionaries and presently has 3,000 long-term workers. Over 100 mission boards have been founded by missionaries who began with OM.

Francis Xavier (1506-1552) was a Spanish, Roman Catholic Jesuit missionary to India, Indonesia, Japan, and briefly to China. He saw hundreds become Christians in India and Japan. Xavier helped in the founding of the Jesuits which Stephen Neill says was "perhaps the most important event in the missionary history of the Roman Catholic Church." He helped awaken Europe to the need for world missions.

(1867-1952) known as the "Apostle to Islam," Zwemer became a leader in the student volunteer movement, helped form the American Arabian Mission and was a member of the Reformed Church in America Mission Board. He founded a journal, the Moslem (now Muslim) World and edited it for 37 years. Zwemer served in the Arabian Gulf and in Egypt and traveled throughout the Muslim world for most of the 38 years (1890-1929). He authored some 29 books and co-authored 19.

Suggestions for Further Reading

> Knowledge precedes interest. Interest precedes action; therefore we are
> responsible first of all, to know.   —Attributed to C. I. Scofield

William Carey had to hand-make a world map to hang above his cobbler's bench in order to learn about and pray for the countries of the world. Today, however, is a wonderful day to learn about missions. Bookshelves fill up every year with new books to help us understand God's plan and our part in fulfilling the Great Commission.

The Holy Spirit normally does not work in a vacuum. We are all born with a vacuum of information about this world, and we gradually fill some of it. If we do not know the name of the capital of a country or where a country is located, the Holy Spirit probably will not call us there or use us to help reach that country or people group.

The following books are a select few that might be of help to you in further learning about missions. (Although each is warmly recommended, the author does not vouch for every view or detail within them.) Many (but not all) of these books are popular, easy to read and in print.

Anthropology

Hiebert, Paul G. *Anthropological Reflections on Missiological Issues.* Grand Rapids: Baker Books, 1994. Hiebert provides a deep textbook uniting theology, anthropology and missions to confront contemporary problems facing missions.

Hiebert, Paul G. *Cultural Anthropology,* 2nd ed. Grand Rapids: Baker Book House, 1983. Cultural Anthropology, written by a master missionary anthropologist, is basic for a missionary's understanding of his or her people.

Kraft, Charles, *Anthropology for Christian Witness.* Mary Knoll, New York: Orbis Books, 1997. Although you may not agree with all that Kraft writes, there still is much helpful material in his works.

Mayers, Marvin K. *Christianity Confronts Culture: A Strategy for Cross-Cultural Evangelism.* Grand Rapids: Zondervan Publishing House, 1974. Mayers' textbook/workbook can help prepare a missionary for understanding the host culture and sharing the Savior within it.

Richardson, Don. *Eternity in their Hearts: The Untold Story of Christianity Among Folk Religions of Ancient People.* Ventura, CA: Regal Books, 1981. Richardson provides a fascinating study of how God has revealed something of Himself in the hearts of people all over our globe.

Smith, Donald K. *Creating Understanding: A Handbook for Christian Communication Across Cultural Landscapes.* Grand Rapids: Zondervan Publishing House, 1992. Smith practices what he preaches and clearly communicates how to communicate across cultures.

Biblical Theology of Missions

Allen, Roland. *Missionary Methods: St. Paul's or Ours?* Grand Rapids, MI: William B. Eerdmans Publishing Co., 1962. Allen first wrote this provocative work in 1912 and it keeps asking disturbing questions.

Kaiser, Walter. *Mission in the Old Testament: Israel as a Light to the Nations.* Grand Rapids: Baker Book House, 2000. A leading Old Testament scholar and president of Gordon Conwell Seminary shows how the Great Commission flows throughout the Old Testament.

Kane, Herbert J. *Christian Missions in Biblical Perspective.* Grand Rapids: Baker Book House, 1976. Kane provides a thorough study of missions in the Bible.

Larkin Jr., William J. and Williams, Joel F. ed. *Mission in the New Testament: An Evangelical Approach.* Maryknoll, NY: Orbis Books, 1998. A deep anthology by graduate professors at Columbia International University.

McQuilkin, Robertson. *The Great Omission: A Biblical Basis for World Evangelism: Why Do So Few Take the Gospel to the Unevangelized?* rev. ed. Waynesboro, GA: Gabriel Publishing, 1984. McQuilkin, a previous president of Columbia International University, addresses a root question.

Peters, W. George. *A Biblical Theology of Missions.* Chicago: Moody Press, 1972. Peters work is a fairly deep study of the teaching of the Word of God on missions.

Piper, John. *Let the Nations be Glad: The Supremacy of God in Missions.* Grand Rapids: Baker Books, 1993. One of the first books to read in learning about bringing the glory of God to the nations.

Schreiner, Thomas R. *Paul, Apostle of God's Glory in Christ: A Pauline Theology.* Downers Grove, IL: InterVarsity Press, 2001. A profound study of Pauline theology with with its missions foundation.

Biography

Crossman, Eileen Fraser. *Mountain Rain: A Biography of James O. Fraser: Pioneer Missionary to China.* Wheaton: Harold Shaw Publishers, 1994. When J. O. Fraser began working with the Lisu peoples, few were believers. In 1916 and 1917 Fraser baptized 60,000 Lisu. Today about 300,000 out of 715,000 are believers in Christ.

Curry, Dayna and Mercer, *Heather with Mattingly, Stacy. Prisoners of Hope: The Story of our Captivity and Freedom in Afghanistan.* NY: Random House, 2002. For those interested in contemporary, young missionaries, the story of Dayna and Heather can make excellent reading.

Edwards, Jonathan. *The Life and Diary of David Brainerd.* Chicago: Moody Press, 1949. Brainerd's life, reaching indigenous North Americans, provides spiritual motivation for any who will read it.

Elliot, Elisabeth. *A Chance to Die: The Life and Legacy of Amy Carmichael.* Old Tappan, NJ: Fleming H. Revell, 1987. Without a furlough for 53 years in India, Amy Carmichael rescued girls from forced temple prostitution and raised them in her Dohnavur Fellowship.

Elliot, Elisabeth. *Shadow of the Almighty: The Life and Testament of Jim Elliot.* San Francisco: Harper & Row, Publishers, 1958. This is one of the first books anyone should read who is considering missions.

Ilaim. *What is That in Your Hand?* revised ed. Reading, PA: Christar, 2004. This contains some of the 646 stories of Muslim background believers in Christ led to Him by a single woman.

Mangalwaqdi, Vishal and Ruth. *The Legacy of William Carey: A Model for the Transformation of a Culture*. Wheaton: Crossway Books, 1999. There are many biographies of the father of modern missions. The Mangalwaqdis concentrate on his contributions.

Miller, William McElwee. *My Persian Pilgrimage: An Autobiography*. revised ed. Pasadena: William Carey Library, 1995. Few of us today can imagine the challenges and joys of Dr. Miller's 43 years in Iran. Well worth reading.

Swift, Catherine. *Eric Liddell: God's Athlete*. Basingstoke, Hanks, UK: Marshall Pickering, 1986. The exciting biography of Eric Liddell, the hero of "Chariots of Fire." Liddell, an MK from and missionary to China, set a world record and won a gold medal in the 1924 Olympics.

Wilson, Dorothy Clarke. *Ten Fingers for God: The Life and Work of Paul Brand*. Grand Rapids: Zondervan, 1989. For those considering medical missions the life of Dr. Paul Brand is a great place to begin.

Church Planting

Garrison, David. *Church Planting Movements*. Richmond, VA: International Mission Board of the Southern Baptist Convention, n.d. Garrison asks, not just how to plant one church, but how to plant a movement of many churches within a people group.

Hesselgrave, David. J. *Planting Churches Cross-Culturally: North America and Beyond*, 2nd ed. Grand Rapids: Baker Books, 2000. Hesselgrave's work is a classic in helping one understand the process.

Livingstone, Greg. *Planting Churches in Muslim Cities: A Team Approach*. Grand Rapids: Baker Book House, 1993. For those desirous of planting fellowships of believers from Muslim backgrounds, Livingstone's work is required reading.

Samson, Wolfgang. *Houses that Change the World: The Return of the House Churches*. Waynesboro, G. A. Paternoster, 2001. Church planting among the least-reached, creative-access peoples usually requires house churches as in the New Testament.

Steffen, Tom A. *Passing the Baton: Church Planting that Empowers*. LaHabra, CA: Center for Organizational and Ministry Development, 1997. Steffen begins with the end in mind, asking how should we finish the church-planting process and then asking what should be done to get there.

Dealing with Issues, Struggles and Fears

Danielson, Edward E. *Missionary Kid (MK)*. Manila, Philippines: Faith Academy, 1982. Danielson, a clinical psychologist who served MKs at the world's largest MK school, helps MKs and their parents prepare for an exciting life on the mission field.

Foyle, Marjory F. *Overcoming Missionary Stress*, Wheaton: Evangelical Missions Information Service, 1987. Foyle, one of the few psychiatrists who helps missionaries full-time, clarifies many of the challenges and some of the solutions affecting missionaries.

Griffiths, Michael C. *Give Up Your Small Ambitions: What You've Always Wanted to Know About Becoming a Missionary*. Chicago: Moody Press, 1979. While providing steps to the field, Griffiths helps address issues, fears and hang-ups faced by those God is calling to missions.

Jones, Marge with Jones, E. Grant. *Psychology of Missionary Adjustment*. Springfield, Missouri: Logion Press, 1995. Jones and Jones provide a very practical preparation for adjustments most missionaries will face.

Lingenfelter, Sherwood G. and Mayers, Marvin. *Ministering Cross Culturally: An Incarnational Model for Personal Relationships*. Grand Rapids: Baker Book House, 1986. Getting along with fellow missionaries is one of our hardest adjustments. Lingenfelter and Mayers provide some needed help.

Long, W. Meredith. *Health, Healing and God's Kingdom. New Pathways to Christian Health Ministry in Africa*. Irvine, CA: Regnum Books International, 2000. Long's work is a helpful place to begin for those interested in how they can use their medical skills on the mission field.

Loss, Myron. Culture Shock: *Dealing with Stress in Cross-Cultural Living*. Winona Lake, IN. Light and Life Press, 1983. We all face culture shock when we work cross-culturally. Loss braces us for the challenge.

Taylor, William D., ed. *Too Valuable to Lose: Exploring the Causes and Cures of Missionary Attrition*. Pasadena, CA: William Carey Library, 1997. Taylor and friends provide a useful study for mission agencies, missionaries and prospective missionaries in understanding some of the challenges and options for prevention or coping with them.

Troutman, Charles. *Everything You Want to Know About the Mission Field, But Are Afraid You Won't Learn Until You Get There: Letters to a Prospective Missionary*. Downers Grove: InterVarsity Press, 1977. Troutman addresses questions asked by each generation of prospective missionaries.

Yep, Jeanette; Cha, Peter; Van Riesen, Susan Cho; Jao, Greg and Tokunaga, Paul. *Following Jesus Without Dishonoring Your Parents: Written by an Asian American Team*. Downers Grove, IL: InterVarsity Press, 1998. An Asian-American team studies a challenge to missions which is not unique to them.

Finances and Missions

Barnett, Betty. *Friend Raising: Building a Missionary Support Team that Lasts*. Seattle: YWAM Publishing, 1991. Barnett shares what she teaches and practices internationally.

Bonk, Jonathan. *Missions and Money: Affluence as a Western Missionary Problem*. Maryknoll, NY: Orbis Books, 1991. Bonk asks how the comparative wealth of the missionary in contrast to many nationals, can harm our message.

Dillon, William P. *People Raising: A Practical Guide to Raising Support*. Chicago: Moody Press, 1993. An interactive step-by-step study that can encourage future missionaries in this important ministry.

Engel, James F. *A Clouded Future? Advancing North American World Missions*. Milwaukee, WI: Christian Stewardship Association, 1996. Engel discusses the challenges and some solutions for financing world mission.

Getting from Here to There

Bacon, Daniel W. *Equipping for Missions: A Guide to Making Career Decisions.* Littleton, CO: OMF International, 1992. Bacon, while the US Director of OMF, prepared an interactive manual to help you find out if missions is for you and if so, to learn steps of preparation.

Hoke, Steve & Taylor, Bill. *Send Me! Your Journey to the Nations.* Pasadena: William Carey Library, 1999. If you want practical steps to explore your preparation for missions, Hoke and Taylor have prepared a prescription that works.

History of Missions

Latourette, Kenneth Scott. *A History of the Expansion of Christianity.* 7 vols. Grand Rapids: Zondervan Publishing House, 1970. If you are looking for details of mission history, Latourette's seven volume work is a must.

Philip Jenkins. *The Next Christendom: The Coming of Global Christianity.* New York: Oxford University Press, 2002. Jenkins, a Penn State University professor, shares detailed insight into the more recent history of Christianity and its spread, even though his book primarily deals with the future of world Christianity.

Tucker, Ruth A. *From Jerusalem to Irian Jaya: A Biographical History of Christian Missions.* Grand Rapids: Zondervan Publishing House, 1983. Tucker's wonderful history of missions is foundational reading.

Introduction to Missions

Hale, Thomas. *On Being a Missionary.* Pasadena: William Carey Library, 2000. For many, Hale's work has become a standard introduction to missions. He shares ideas from over 100 missionary authors.

Kane, J. Herbert. *Life and Work on the Mission Field.* Grand Rapids: Baker Book House, 1980. Kane's work remains one of the best first steps in learning about the mission field, from receiving a call until furlough.

Olson, C. Gordon. *What in the World is God Doing?: The Essentials of Global Missions: An Introductory Guide.* Cedar Knolls, NJ: Global Gospel Publishers, 1989. Gordon Olson's introduction to missions has been a standard textbook in over 100 colleges and seminaries.

Van Rheenen, Gailyn. *Missions: Biblical Foundations and Contemporary Strategies.* Grand Rapids: Zondervan Publishing House, 1996. This is a useful place to begin in learning about missions today.

Verwer, George. *Out of the Comfort Zone: A Compelling Vision for Transforming Global Missions.* Minneapolis: Bethany House, 2000. Verwer's passion as the master mobilizer for missions comes through clearly.

Winter, Ralph D. and Hawthorne, Steven C., eds. *Perspectives on the World Christian Movement: A Reader.* Pasadena: William Carey Library, 1999. A foundational reader with many chapters by a variety of mission leaders.

The Local Church and Missions

ACMC Church Missions Policy Handbook, 3rd ed. Peachtree City: ACMC, 1995 Advancing Churches in Missions Commitment, previously Association of Church Missions Committees, has produced a thorough handbook to help a church's mission committee think through their policies on sixty-five different issues with numerous options for each question.

Mays, David, *How to Get Your Congregation Involved in Missions*. Atlanta: ACMC, 1997. David Mays, the Great Lakes Regional Director of ACMC, shares numerous proven ideas to awaken and strengthen a church's passion for God's passion.

Telford, Tom with Shaw, Lois. *Today's All-Star Missions Churches: Strategies to Help Your Church Get into the Game*. Grand Rapids: Baker Books, 2001. Telford shares his careful research into churches around the U.S. who are doing a significant work in mobilizing their fellowships to bring the gospel around the world.

Telford, Tom with Shaw, Lois. *Missions in the 21st Century: Getting Your Church into the Game*, Charlotte: United World Mission, 1998. Tom Telford, the head coach for helping churches and church mission committees in missions, shares what he has learned from 26 years of mentoring hundreds of churches.

Rowell, John. *Magnify Your Vision for the Small Church*. Atlanta: Northside Community Church, 1998. John Rowell explains how Northside Community Church, with 250 to 450 people, has been used by God to begin a church planting movement among Muslims in Bosnia. www.acmc.org There is a wealth of information to help a local church's mission program on ACMC's site.

Is Christ the Only Way?

Carson, D. A. *The Gagging of God: Christianity Confronts Pluralism*. Grand Rapids: Zondervan, 1966. In his deep biblical and theological work Carson provides helpful understanding of the uniqueness of Christ in a pluralistic age and thoughtful responses to those who deny the reality and duration of hell.

Cate, Patrick O. *The Uniqueness of Christ and Missions*. This paper was originally prepared for IFMA and EMS and can be found at www.christar.org. It is a study of the uniqueness of Christ and the reality of hell in the context of our tolerant, diverse, pluralistic and post-modern age. It addresses the question, "Is Christ truly the only way of salvation?"

Fernando, Ajith. *The Supremacy of Christ*. Wheaton: Crossway Books, 1995. The majority of believers in Christ are non-Westerners and Fernando is an outstanding example. Those of us in the West can profit from their thinking and his in particular.

Kennedy, D. James. *Evangelism Explosion*, 4th ed. Wheaton: Tyndale House Publishers, 1966. pp. 162-166. James Kennedy's church has grown from 17 to 9,000 members using Evangelism Explosion methods. He has specialized in addressing the questions of a seeker.

Lutzer, Erwin W. *Christ Among Other gods: A Defense of Christ in An Age of Tolerance*. Chicago: Moody Press, 1994. Coming out of the 1993 Parliament of the World's Religions, Lutzer writes from a careful popular approach to a subject which daily affects us.

Netland, Harold A. *Dissonant Voices: Religious Pluralism and the Question of Truth*. Vancouver, British Columbia: Regent College Publishing, 1991. Netland provides a scholarly study on the uniqueness of Christ versus the philosophical pluralism of our day.

Netland, Harold A. *Encountering Religious Pluralism: The Challenge to Christian Faith and Mission*. Downers Grove, IL: InterVarsity Press, 2001. Deep evangelical philosophical responses are articulated by Netland to one of the central threats facing missions today.

Sanders, J. Oswald. *What of Those Who Have Never Heard*. Crowborough, East Sussex: Highland Books, 1966. This is a thoughtful overview, with Sanders analyzing numerous facets of the question.

Strobel, Lee. *The Case for Faith*. Grand Rapids: Zondervan, 2000. pp. 145-194. Strobel combines his penetrating legal mind with experienced journalistic skills to get to root challenges of Christian faith.

Zacharias, Ravi. *Jesus Among Other Gods: The Absolute Claims of the Christian Message*. Nashville: Word Publishing, 2000. Brilliant, Indian born Zacharias digs into a foundational issue in missions.

Journals

Evangelical Missions Quarterly. (www.wheaton.edu/bgc/emis) If you can only subscribe to one missions journal, EMQ is the one.

International Bulletin of Missionary Research (www.OMSC.org) The Overseas Ministry Study Center publishes insightful scholarly articles from Roman Catholic, conciliar, charismatic and evangelical persuasions.

The International Journal of Frontier Missions (e-mail: ijfm@wciu.edu) . The IJFM provides articles on reaching the least-reached, sometimes in a deeper way than Missions Frontiers.

Missiology: An International Review (www.asmweb.org/missiology.htm) An academic journal published by the American Society of Missiology from Roman Catholic, conciliar and evangelical perspectives.

Missions Frontiers. (www.uscwm.org) Missions Frontiers, published by the U.S. Center for World Missions, specializes in pioneer, least-reached type of missions.

World Pulse. (www.wheaton,edu/bgc/emis) A helpful monthly source of worldwide mission news.

Language Learning

Brown, H. Douglas. *Breaking the Language Barrier*. Yarmouth, ME: Intercultural Press, 1991. Brown's work is geared for those studying in a classroom and can also be used for self-directed learning. Through a non-technical style Brown provides motivation which most language learners need.

Marshall, Terry. *The Whole World Guide to Language Learning*. Yarmouth, ME: Intercultural Press, 1989. Written for independent language learners, it describes the learning cycle of LAMP and Becoming Bilingual.

Moran, P.R. Lexicarry, *Pro Lingua*, 1990. Brattleboro, VT. This is an illustrated vocabulary builder for a second language acquisition and is considered the best picture dictionary available.

The Rosetta Stone. The Rosetta Stone is software for many languages useful before a person goes to the field to help them develop comprehension. If you purchase it through www.Wheaton.edu/bgc/ICCT or through www.mti.org, you can obtain a missionary discount.

Rubin, J. and Thompson, I. *How to Be A More Successful Language Learner*. Heinle & Heinle, 1994. If you can only read one book on learning a second language, begin with this one. This is the place to begin for an overview of what you need to know for acquiring a second language.

SIL. *LinguaLinks Language Learning Bookshelf*. LinguaLinks Library (1999). This is a very useful CD-ROM produced by the Summer Institute of Linguistics. This provides a variety of material to help a language learner. This CD is updated twice a year and may be ordered through www.sil.org.

Mission Web Sites

www.acmc.org There is a wealth of information to help a local church's missions program on the site of Advancing Churches in Missions Commitment.

www.answering-islam.org Answering-Islam is a primary source in learning how to share Christ's love with Muslims and how to help Muslims with questions they may have.

www.askamissionary.com Offers questions and answers for those considering long-term missions.

www.brigada.org Brigada provides a weekly e-mail journal of current trends, resources and motivation for missions.

www.calebproject.org The Caleb project offers helpful research on the unreached and how to get connected.

www.GlobalMission.org. The official site of the World Evangelical Alliance Missions Commission includes the largest data base of mission organizations around the world plus many long and short-term opportunities worldwide.

www.gmi.org Global Mapping International provides an excellent source of maps and links for mission research.

www.mislinks.org Scott Moreau of Wheaton Graduate School has produced a web-based directory of numerous resources helpful for those interested in missions from the entry level to the scholar.

www.missiology.org Missions professor Van Rheenen's web site includes a missions dictionary, material on animism, bibliographies and mission quotations.

www.SIL.org SIL's ethnologue catalogues 6800 languages spoken in 231 countries.

www.Strategicnetwork.org Justin Long of World Christian Encyclopedia has more than 10,000 articles on missions and the back issues of major mission journals, and has 23,000 subscribers to its interactive e-groups.

www.Wheaton.edu/bgc/ICCT The Institute for Cross-Cultural Training (ICCT) has produced an outstanding web site for language learning resources and links, especially for a missionary.

www.worldskip.com Worldskip provides a vast amount of information on every country in the world for a cost of $12 per year

Needs of the World

Barrett, David and Johnson, Todd. *World Christian Trends, AD30-AD2200: Interpreting the Annual Christian Mega Census.* Pasadena: William Carey Library, 2001. The authors of the World Christian Encyclopedia spell out detailed needs and trends of our world.

Johnstone, Patrick. *The Church is Bigger Than You Think: The Unfinished Work of World Evangelism.* Ross-shire, UK: Christian Focus Publishers, 1998. Johnstone's wisdom comes out as he shares practical ramifications from his classic, Operation World.

Johnstone, Patrick and Mandryk, Jason. *Operation World: When We Pray God Works.* 21st century ed. Waynesboro, GA: Paternoster USA, 2001. Ralph Winters says this is the second most important book for any Christian to own and read. It provides a digest of facts and prayer requests for each of the 237 states and territories in the world.

Persecution

Marshall, Paul. *Their Blood Cries Out: The Untold Story of Persecution Against Christians in the Modern World.* Dallas: Word Publishing, 1997. In the West we have frequently become isolated from the persecution that many Christians of the world face.

Rogers, Charles and Sytsma, Brian. *World Vision Security Manual: Safety Awareness for Aid Workers.* Geneva, Switzerland: World Vision, 1999. World Vision has prepared one of the most practical books to avoid and cope with terrorism and persecution.

Shea, Nina. *In the Lion's Den: A Shocking Account of Persecution and Martyrdom of Christians Today and How We Should Respond.* Nashville: Broadman and Holman Publishers, 1997. Shea addresses one of the most important issues facing missionaries today.

Talk, dc and The Voice of the Martyrs. *Jesus Freaks: Stories of Those Who Stood for Jesus: The Ultimate Jesus Freaks.* Tulsa, OK: Albury Publishing, 1999. These stories of ordinary Christians who gave their lives for Christ in martyrdom from ancient times to the present day, speak to our chaotic world.

Ton, Joseph. *Suffering, Martyrdom and Rewards in Heaven.* Wheaton: The Romanian Bible Society, 2000. An excellent doctoral dissertation studying Scripture and church history on suffering martyrdom and rewards by a Romanian who preached and taught for nearly a decade, realizing suffering and martyrdom could be imminent.

Prayer and Fasting

Hawthorne, Steve. *Prayer-Walking: Praying On Site with Insight.* Creation House, 1993. Prayer walks have been used by God to see cities reached and lives changed.

Johnstone, Patrick and Mandryk, Jason. *Operation World: When We Pray God Works.* 21st century ed. Waynesboro, GA: Paternoster USA, 2001. Operation World is the best single source of prayer requests for the 237 states and territories in the world.

Piper, John. *A Hunger for God: Desiring God through Fasting and Prayer.* Wheaton: Crossway Books, 1997. A helpful study on fasting and desiring God more than food.

Wagner, C. Peter. *Prayer: How to Intercede for Pastors, Christian Leaders and Others on the Spiritual Front Lines.* Ventura, CA: Regal, 1992. Wagner has written an excellent introduction to prayer, useful for those going to the mission field.

Role of Women

Cate, Mary Ann and Sue Eenigenburg, ed. *A Woman's Touch: A Guide for Women in Cross-Cultural Ministry.* rev. Reading, PA: Christar, 2001. When language study is over many women ask, "What do I do now?" A Woman's Touch is one of the best tools available to enable younger women to learn answers from older women.

Cate, Mary Ann and Karol Downey, ed. *From Fear to Faith: Muslim and Christian Women.* Pasadena: William Carey Library, 2002. An excellent resource from the Second Consultation on Ministry to Muslim Women to better enable Christian women to reach Muslim women.

Love, Fran and Eckheart, Jeleta, ed. *Ministry to Muslim Women: Longing to Call them Sisters.* Pasadena; William Carey Library, 2000. The first Consultation on Ministry to Muslim Women produced this anthology of articles relevant to reaching Muslim women.

Tucker, Ruth A. *Guardians of the Great Commission: The Story of Women in Modern Missions.* Grand Rapids: Zondervan Publishing House, 1988. Tucker's biographical history of heroines of the gospel helps to understand the joys and challenges of women missionaries.

Spiritual Warfare

Horton, Michael Scott, ed. *Power Religions: The Selling Out of the Evangelical Church.* Chicago: Moody Press, 1992. A variety of evangelical scholars ask for careful and biblical thinking related to the contemporary emphasis on power encounters and power ministries.

Pirolo, Neal and Yvonne. *Prepare for Battle: Basic Training in Spiritual Warfare.* San Diego, CA: Emmaus Road, International, 1997. The Pirolos point out that remembering the basics can bring victory in our spiritual battles.

Rommen, Edward, ed. *Spiritual Power and Missions: Raising the Issues.* Pasadena, CA: William Carey Library, 1995. The writers clarify some of the issues affecting spiritual warfare, missions and prayer.

Warner, Timothy W. *Spiritual Warfare: Victory Over the Powers of This Dark World.* Wheaton: Crossway Books, 1991. Warner provides a fairly balanced approach to help in our warfare.

Trends Affecting Missions

Barrett, David and Johnson, Todd. *World Christian Trends, AD 30-AD2200: Interpreting the Annual Christian Mega Census*. Pasadena: William Carey Library, 2001. The authors of the exhaustive World Christian Encyclopedia share their wisdom and interpretation of this massive data.

Dryness, William A. *Learning about Theology from the Third World*. Grand Rapids: Zondervan Publishing House, 1990. Those of us who are Westerners at times need to take off our Western glasses and put on Third World glasses to better understand our calling.

Guthrie, Stan. *Missions in the Third Millennium: Key Trends for the 21st Century*. Waynesboro, GA: Send the Light Paternoster, 1999. From Guthrie's journalistic background in missions, he has acquired insight into many important trends affecting missions.

Lundy, David. *We Are the World: Globalization and the Changing Face of Missions*. Cumbrian, UK: Paternoster Publishing, 1999. The internationalization and globalization of missions is one of the most significant trends today, and Lundy provides one of the best studies of it.

Phillips, James M. and Coots, Robert T. eds. *Toward the 21st Century in Christian Mission*. Grand Rapids, MI: William B. Eerdmans Publishing Company, 1993. Numerous scholars look at a variety of issues facing missions in this century.

World Religions

Cordvan, Winfried. *Neighboring Faiths: A Christian Introduction to World Religions*. Downers Grove, IL: InterVarsity Press, 1998. Among the numerous introductions to world religions, this one is a great place to start.

Noss, David S. *A History of the World's Religions*. 10th ed. Upper Saddle River, NJ: Prentice Hall, 1994. Noss, and his brother John, have authored a detailed textbook used in over 700 educational institutions.

Ro, Bong Rin. *Christian Alternatives to Ancestor Practices*. Taichung, Taiwan: Asian Theological Association, 1985. Christians working among Chinese and Buddhists frequently say that ancestor worship is their biggest theological challenge.

Saal, William. *Reaching Muslims for Christ*. Chicago: Moody Press, 1991. The number of books and articles on Islam increases geometrically. Saal's work is a helpful place to begin.

Tennet, Timothy C. *Christianity at the Religious Round Table: Evangelism in Conversation with Hinduism, Buddhism and Islam*. Grand Rapids, MI: Baker Academic, 2002. Tennet provides an insightful study into the dialogue between world religions.

Thirumalai, Madasamy. *Sharing Your Faith with a Hindu*. Minneapolis: Bethany House, 2002. There is a fair amount written on Hinduism but little on how to reach Hindus for Christ and so Thirumalai provides a useful foundation.

Van Rheenen, Gailyn. *Communicating Christ in Animistic Contexts*. Pasadena: William Carey Library, 1996. In addition to pure animists or tribal peoples, animism pervades each religious culture. Van Rheenen helps us understand animism and take steps to reach them.

Weerasingha, Tissa. *The Cross and the Bo Tree: Communicating the Gospel to Buddhists.* Taichung, Taiwan: Asian Theological Association, 1989. This is one of the few quality books to help in reaching Buddhists.

About Christar (formerly International Missions, Inc.)

Bringing Light to the Least-Reached

Mission Statement

The mission of Christar is to glorify God by establishing churches, primarily within least-reached Buddhist, Hindu, Muslim and Asian communities worldwide. In this endeavor, we partner with churches to send out missionaries who proclaim the gospel and equip the body of Christ.

Vision Statement

The vision of Christar is to see more churches planted among more of the least-reached through effective prayer, growing people, godly teams and fruitful partnerships.

Values

In Christar we value Godliness, the body of Christ, personal development, effectiveness and creativity.

Prayer-based: Christar asks its missionaries to find 100 people who will pray for them daily before they go to the mission field. We are engaged in spiritual warfare and spiritual warfare is won on our knees. We unite in daily, weekly, monthly and yearly seasons of prayer. God, in His wonderful kindness, keeps answering prayer in over 25 countries.

Innovative: Christar focuses on the neediest people, those with the least opportunity to hear of Jesus Christ. In Christar we reach people in the 10/40 Window and from the 10/40 Window. We reach Asians internationally. In other words, we reach the least-reached people in their home countries, and we reach them as minorities where they emigrate.

Christar is biblical in its theology and progressive in its methodology. Decisions about children's schooling are primarily the parents' responsibility. Areas of women's ministry have been pioneered by Christar through our Department of Women's Ministry where experienced women mentor and encourage younger women. We believe a zest for living is the by-product of all that God calls us to do.

Experienced: Our 90 plus years in the 10/40 Window could be of help when the going gets tough. The stability of reaching Chinese/Buddhists since 1909 and Hindus and Muslims since 1930 provides experience and maturity which helps new missionaries catch the baton and keep from faltering as they trust the Lord and reach those least-reached with the gospel of Jesus Christ.

Tentmaking: Half of our countries are creative-access countries which do not offer missionary visas but which do need secular skills such as teaching English as a second language, medicine, education, agriculture, business, engineering and other skills and professions. We use secular skills to obtain visas into creative-access countries and to obtain visas into hearts closed off from the gospel.

Teams: Each of us serves God together with believers who have other spiritual gifts to plant the Body of Christ where it does not exist. We are led by servant leaders who are player/coaches. Christar is a family which desires to care for its own; we do not send out missionaries as lone rangers to sink or swim. We are there to serve our people.

Board of Trustees

Jeff Adams, Senior Pastor, Kansas City Baptist Temple, MO

Virgil Amos, Founder and President of Ambassadors Fellowship, CO

Samuel Barkat, Psychologist, Educator, Consultant, NY

David J. Baseler, Retired VP ServiceMaster, NC

Keith Carlson, Esq., Attorney, NJ

Patrick O. Cate, President, Christar, PA

John D. Deakins, Founder and President of Christian Business Leaders, Inc., CO

Scott Holbrook, CFO Avant Ministries, MO

Peter Hwang, Pastor, First Korean Baptist Church of Philadelphia, PA

Stephen Kegerise, CPA, PA

Robert Kennedy, Dean, Michigan Theological Seminary, MI

G. Robert Kilgore, Chairman, Professor, Philadelphia Biblical University, PA

Johnny V. Miller, Pastor, Calvary Church, Lancaster, PA

Marvin Newell, Professor of Missions, Moody Bible Institute Graduate School, IL

C. Gordon Olson, Trustee Emeritus, Professor and Author, NJ

Greg H. Parsons, Executive Director, US Center for World Mission, CA

Thomas Turbiak, Physician, CT

Women's Advisory Council

Mary Ann Cate, Director of Women's Ministries, Christar, PA

Kyeong-Sook Park, Professor Moody Bible Institute, IL

Earlene Voss, Missionary-at-Large, Christar, NY

Canadian Board of Trustees

Glenn Birch, Government Administrator, Chairman, ON

Patrick O. Cate, President, Christar, PA

Wayne Harnden, Pastor, ON

Kenneth Hoffman, Secretary, Christar, PA

Carol Potratz, Administrator, North American Baptist Mission Board, IL

Kevin Schular, Pastor, ON

Daniel B. Smith, Pastor, ON

Council of Reference

Miriam Adeney, Seattle Pacific University, Teaching Fellow; Regent College, WA, Assistant Professor

Joseph Aldrich, President Emeritus, Multnomah Bible College and Biblical Seminary, OR

Hudson T. Amerding, President Emeritus, Wheaton College, IL

A. Jean Barsness, Retired Educator, CANADA

J. Ronald Blue, Professor, Dallas Theological Seminary, TX

D. Stuart Briscoe, Pastor-at-Large, Elmbrook Church, WI

Luis Bush, Founder AD2000 & Beyond, VA

Howard G. Hendricks, Distinguished Professor, Chairman of the Center for Christian Leadership, Dallas Theological Seminary, TX

David Hesselgrave, Professor Emeritus of Missions, Trinity Evangelical Divinity School, IL

Patrick Johnstone, Researcher/Author, WEC, U.K.

Robertson J. McQuilkin, Chancellor, Columbia International University, SC

Abel E. Morales, President FAM International, Guatemala

Haddon W. Robinson, Professor, Gordon-Conwell Theological Seminary, MA

Joseph M. Stowell, President, Moody Bible Institute, IL

George Verwer, Founder of Operation Mobilisation, U.K.

For information, questions, opportunities or missionary vocational counseling, contact:

Box 14866, Reading, PA 19612 · (800) 755-7955 (610) 375-0300 · Fax: (610) 375-6862 · Email: info@christar.org

Box 20164, St. Catharines, ON L2M 7W7 · (800) 295-4158 (905) 646-0228 · Fax: (905) 646-0228 · Email: imont@npiec.on.ca

P.O. Box 656, Shatin Post Office, Shatin, NT Hong Kong · +852 2602 0355 · fax +852 2900 9087 · info@christar-hk.com

www.christar.org